W9-BGS-828

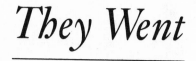

# They Went

*The Writer's Craft*
*William Zinsser, Series Editor*

EXTRAORDINARY LIVES
*The Art and Craft of American Biography*

INVENTING THE TRUTH
*The Art and Craft of Memoir*

SPIRITUAL QUESTS
*The Art and Craft of Religious Writing*

PATHS OF RESISTANCE
*The Art and Craft of the Political Novel*

WORLDS OF CHILDHOOD
*The Art and Craft of Writing for Children*

THEY WENT
*The Art and Craft of Travel Writing*

# *They Went*

## THE ART AND CRAFT
## OF TRAVEL WRITING

IAN FRAZIER

ANDREA LEE

MARK SALZMAN

VIVIAN GORNICK

CALVIN TRILLIN

TOBIAS SCHNEEBAUM

*Edited by* WILLIAM ZINSSER

HOUGHTON MIFFLIN COMPANY

BOSTON

Introduction copyright © 1991 William K. Zinsser. "Carving Your Name on the Rock" copyright © 1991 Ian Frazier. "Double Lives" copyright © 1991 Andrea Lee. "Peopling the Landscape" copyright © 1991 Mark Salzman. "An American Woman in Egypt" copyright © 1991 Vivian Gornick. "Traveling in America" copyright © 1991 Calvin Trillin. "A Drive into the Unknown" copyright © 1991 Tobias Schneebaum.

Library of Congress Cataloging-in-Publication Data

They went : the art and craft of travel writing / Ian Frazier . . . [et al.] ; edited by William Zinsser.
p.    cm. — (The Writer's craft)
"Originated as a series of talks held at the New York Public Library in winter of 1990" —
Includes bibliographical references.
I S B N 0–395–56336–4    I S B N 0–395–56337–2 (pbk.)
1. Travel — Authorship.    I. Zinsser, William Knowlton.
II. Series.
G151.T48    1991
808'.0669 — dc20                    90–5366
C I P

Three passages in Calvin Trillin's "Traveling in America" originally appeared in *The New Yorker* as "U.S. Journal: Jeremiah, Kentucky: A Stranger with a Camera"; "U.S. Journal: Center Junction, Iowa: Jim, Tex, and the One-armed Man"; "U.S. Journal: Miami Beach: Harvey St. Jean Had It Made" in 1969, 1971, and 1975, respectively.

Excerpt from "The Town That Practices Parading" by Calvin Trillin (TIME, August 22, 1988) is reprinted by permission.

A portion of the Introduction by William Zinsser first appeared in the *New York Times Book Review*, with the title "A Travel Nut's Library."

Printed in the United States of America

HAD 10 9 8 7 6 5 4 3 2 1

# Note

This book originated as a series of talks held at The New York Public Library in the winter of 1990. Five previous series resulted in the books *Extraordinary Lives, Inventing the Truth, Spiritual Quests, Paths of Resistance* and *Worlds of Childhood*. The publisher would like to thank the Library and its coordinator of public education programs, David Cronin, for the Library's gracious collaboration as host of the series.

# Contents

# Contents

WILLIAM ZINSSER

# *Introduction*

Old travel books occupy so many shelves in my apartment that a visitor might take me to be some kind of antiquarian nut. I'm merely a travel nut, and the books are artifacts of that hobby. Just looking at their sonorous titles (*Forbidden Sands*, *Monsoon Seas*, *Dead Cities and Forgotten Tribes*, *They Reigned in Mandalay*), I'm taken back to places in many parts of the world that I traveled far to see. I'm also reminded of how the books found their way into my life.

I'm not a likely owner, for instance, of *Garden Islands of the Great East: Collecting Seeds from the Philippines and Netherlands India in the Junk "Chêng Ho,"* by David Fairchild; botany isn't a subject I've been accused of boring my friends with. Yet if I take the book down and open it to its endpapers—an illustrated map of the Moluccas, the old Spice Islands of the East Indies, where Dr. Fairchild gathered exotic plants in 1940 for the Fairchild Tropical Garden in Florida—I can see and smell the copra boat that I took through those same Moluccas in 1953, and I think with gratitude of the traveler who urged me to make the trip. That traveler was S. J. Perelman.

Perelman was a licensed humorist practicing his trade when Ted Patrick, editor of *Holiday*, a magazine that elevated travel journalism to literature in the years right after World War II, sent him on two round-the-world trips—one with the artist Al Hirschfeld, the other with his wife Laura and their two children. The pieces that Perelman wrote became the books *Westward Ha!* and *The Swiss Family Perelman*, which also sit on my shelf. But humor is not what I remember when I see them. I remember what a serious traveler those two trips made of Perelman. (Ultimately he went around the world six times.) He fell in love with Southeast Asia, especially Indonesia, and talked about the area with erudition and high enjoyment, his famously esoteric vocabulary now seasoned with Malay words and pompous British colonialisms.

What stuck in his mind most fondly was a voyage he made on a copra boat of the old Dutch K.P.M. line that "hemstitched" its way around the island of

Celebes and the Moluccas, and he recommended it to me as a fellow addict. I duly booked passage on a K.P.M. boat out of Macassar, and he sent me off with the names of various people in the islands he thought I would find helpful. One was an urbane Dutch planter in Surabaya named Daan Hubrecht. He told me he knew the Moluccas well because he had sailed among them as a young man with David Fairchild's plant-collecting voyage on the junk *Chêng Ho*. The junk, he explained, had been specially built in Hong Kong for Dr. Fairchild's expedition, with a modern botanical laboratory below decks, by an American explorer and scientific patron named Anne Archbold. It was modeled on a fifteenth-century Chinese junk, was brightly painted and decorated, and was altogether, he said, quite a sight. He showed me a picture of it in *Garden Islands of the Great East*.

The story got pushed out of my mind by all the other stories I heard on that trip, which lived up to Perelman's promise; I fell in love with Indonesia too. But when I got back home I found myself thinking about that Chinese junk, and I tracked down Dr. Fairchild's book. From the first paragraph I was charmed:

It was sometime in the eighties that Alfred Russel Wallace came to the college in Kansas where my father was President and delivered a lecture on Natural Selection. I was too young to understand what Wallace said on the platform, but I listened intently to his conversation in our house the evening after the lecture. I like to imagine that it was this meeting with the great naturalist which started my longing to see, when I grew up, those islands of the Great East — the Malay Archipelago.

What charmed me was the idea of a boy too young to understand the lecture but not too young to recognize the eminent man on the platform as his model, the exemplar of what would become his own life work. By the time Dr. Fairchild went plant-gathering in the Moluccas he was an old man himself — the jacket photograph on *Garden Islands of the Great East* shows a white-haired gentleman standing on the deck of the *Chêng Ho*. (His wife Marian, who went along, was the daughter of Alexander Graham Bell.) But if there is one work that his book echoes in its warmth and its scholarly curiosity it is Alfred Russel Wallace's mighty classic, *The Malay Archipelago*. Dr. Fairchild's expedition was halted after six months by the outbreak of World War II in the East Indies, but the plants that he collected are alive and well in Florida today. The book didn't say what became of the *Chêng Ho*, and, again, I put it out of my mind.

Three years later, stopping off in Papeete on a trip through the South Seas, I noticed what appeared to be a derelict junk pulled up onto a beach at the far end of the harbor. At that time Tahiti's capital was still a small town, its only air service a seaplane every two weeks, and everyone who hung around the water-front — the town's main occupation — knew every-one else's business. I asked if anybody knew about the junk. Everybody did. It was called the *Chêng Ho*, they said, and it had led a succession of picturesque lives during World War II, serving as, among other things, a radar ship and a naval officers' club in Honolulu. After the war it had fallen into private hands and had been seen in various parts of the South Pacific, finally coming to rest in Papeete.

I suspected that there was more to the story of the *Chêng Ho* than any one teller of tales had put together, and for a while I thought of pursuing it and writing it myself; someone said the *Honolulu Star* had an entire file on it. In the end, however, I let the scent grow faint. Only one person kept it alive, and that was Perelman. He loved the idea of the *Chêng Ho*. I think he wanted to believe that someone like himself had restored it and was sailing it in perpetuity through the Moluccas. A year or two before he died at the age of seventy-five he told me he had been corresponding with a shipbuilder in Hong Kong to see if he could get a junk built that would take him back to Banda. Travelers' destinations don't come much smaller or harder to reach than Banda — a minuscule Spice

Island that Westerners have known since the early 1500s because of its nutmeg. Perelman had gone there in 1949 solely because of what another writer wrote about it. The writer was Somerset Maugham; the book was his novel *The Narrow Corner*.

The bungalows on either side of the road had very high roofs, thatched and pointed, and the roofs, jutting out, were supported by pillars, Doric and Corinthian, so as to form broad verandahs. They had an air of ancient opulence, but their whitewash was stained and worn, and the little gardens in front of them were rank with tangled weeds. They came to shops and they all seemed to sell the same sort of things, cottons, sarongs, and canned foods. There was no animation. Some of the shops had not even an attendant, as though no purchaser could possibly be expected. The few persons they passed, Malays or Chinese, walked quickly as though they were afraid to awaken the echo. Now and then a whiff of nutmeg assaulted the nostrils. . . .

"The place is dead," said Captain Nichols. "We live on our memories. That is what gives the island its character. In the old days, you know, there was so much traffic that sometimes the harbor was full and vessels had to wait outside till the departure of a fleet gave them a chance to enter. . . .

"The old Dutch merchants were so rich here in the great days of the spice trade, they didn't know what to do with their money. There was no cargo for the ships to bring out and so they used to bring marble and use it for their houses. And sometimes, in winter, they'd bring a cargo of nothing but ice. Funny, isn't it? That was the greatest luxury they could have. Just think of bringing ice all the way from Holland. It took six months, the journey."

Perelman was so determined to see those houses that he caught a small boat at Amboina that took him 120 miles through a heavy storm. His cabin was "just high enough for a malnourished orangutan to stand upright in" and he was sustained only by "the sense of accomplishment that springs from lying half dead in a greasy bunk adrift on an alien sea." But when he arrived he was no less astonished than Maugham had been:

We stumbled through a cluster of weedy streets lined with bombed-out dwellings and arrived in due course at an awesome structure resembling a Southern antebellum mansion. This, I was to discover, was one of thirty equally splendid houses built by the Dutch perkeniers, or nutmeg planters, when Banda was at her crest. To convey the magnificence of these establishments without lapsing into the florid style of Ouida or Edgar Saltus is not easy. They all had lofty Corinthian porticoes, reception halls and bedchambers without end, floors of eighteenth-century tile and Carrara marble, servants' quarters, and formal gardens; but more remarkable, they were all available at a ceiling rent of a dollar and fifty cents a month. If the foregoing sounds overly idyllic to anyone caught in a housing shortage, it is well to remember that every rose has its thorn. Banda, no matter what part of the world you live in, is approximately thirteen thousand miles away and a very tough commute.

What I admire about Perelman's account is not the style; it's the effort he made to get there and to write about it. In itself the wealth of white colonials in the East isn't a new story; countless writers have taken us to the posh homes and hill stations of the British raj. But Banda? Who knows about Banda — a microscopic island so rich that its colonial masters were able to build marble mansions and import ice from home? "This I've got to see," Perelman thought, reading Maugham, and he put himself through severe discomfort — as good travel writers will — to see it. But it was Maugham who got there first. The debt is to him.

Indebtedness is at the heart of travel literature. Writing well about a place goes back at least to Herodotus, and the best practitioners usually know and love what has gone before. Travel books, more than most books, get loaned, raved about, handed on. One of the writers Perelman most admired is Norman Lewis — which is how I happen to own *his* book, *A Dragon Apparent: Travels in Indo-China*. It was published in 1951, and I still remember the tranquillity of the Indochinese culture that Lewis evoked; his writer's sensibility and the sensibility of the country were in tune — one of the best things that can happen to a writer and to a country. Today a heavy sadness lies over the book; we have killed Norman Lewis's country. Yet only forty years ago this is how he introduced it at the start of his journey:

The population of the whole of Indo-China is concentrated in a few fertile valleys and deltas, leaving the greater part of the country unpopulated, jungle-covered, and looking much the same as China itself must have looked several thousand years ago, before the deforestation began. The interior is neither completely mapped, nor completely explored. It abounds with game: elephants, tigers, deer and many kinds of cattle, which, having known only hunters armed with cross-bows, may be closely approached and slaughtered with the greatest ease from cars on the jungle tracks. Pacification of the Moïs of Central and Southern Vietnam — those bow and arrow tribes which in the early part of the last century were believed to be the only human beings with tails — was only undertaken in 1934. Certain tribes of the remote interior have not yet submitted to French authority.

Decades of war have made Norman Lewis's book a relic. But when he wrote *A Dragon Apparent* it was true to what he found in Indochina. Beyond the beauty of its language it had the strength of solid observation. Travel writers no less than journalists are prisoners of a particular time and place, and their books are often the last portrait of an intact culture before it was overtaken by events and changed forever. Another such act of preservation on my shelf is a book by Evelyn Waugh called *They Were Still Dancing*. Waugh went to Abyssinia in 1930 to cover the coronation of Haile Selassie and found his reportorial efforts often bogged in what was still a pastoral nineteenth-century kingdom. Anyone reading his book would have known what the newsreels so brutally told the rest of us a few years later when the emperor's foot soldiers tried to resist Mussolini's invading tanks.

After the invasion Waugh recycled his research into a novel, the hilarious *Scoop*, wherein a London newspaper mistakenly sends its nature correspondent to a similarly feudal African country to cover a similarly outlandish war. Whether Waugh's nonfiction version is "truer" than his fiction version is almost beside the point; some of the best travel writing turns up in novels and short stories. Nobody has caught the underside of Los Angeles better than Raymond Chandler in his private-eye novels like *The Big Sleep*, or the tackiness of the American road better than Vladimir Nabokov in *Lolita*, or the claustrophobia of British planters' wives in Malaya better than Maugham in his short stories, or the languor of Italy better than Norman Douglas in *South Wind*.

*South Wind*, which is set on an island easily recognizable as Capri, is the only book by Norman Douglas that anyone but a travel nut remembers — the source of his lasting fame. But I first met him as the author of highly distinctive accounts of his journeys, mostly on foot, to corners of the Mediterranean so plain and primitive — *Old Calabria* is typical — that to want to go there takes a certain perversity. Douglas was a charter member of that breed of British "desert eccentrics" who sought the solitude of harsh places and wrote brilliant books about them. (Pertinent titles on my bookshelf: *Arabia Deserta*, by Charles M. Doughty; *The Seven Pillars of Wisdom*, by T. E. Lawrence; *Riding to the Tigris*, by Freya Stark; *The Last Nomad*, by Wilfred Thesiger; *The Letters of Gertrude Bell*.) The worlds that these restless hermits wrote about were often interior worlds, tinged with mysticism and rumination, and it could hardly have been otherwise. They had reached their destinations by following trails that weren't on any map; part of their genius was that they were a little crazy. But no books remind us more powerfully that what raises travel writing to literature is not what the writer brings to a place, but what a place brings out of the writer. Probably the best travel book written by an American is Thoreau's *Walden*, though the hermit of Concord hardly got beyond the town limits.

My first Norman Douglas book remains vivid in my memory because it's connected with the trip that started my travel habit. The place was North Africa, the period World War II. I was a private in the army, not long sprung from a sheltered boyhood. I had crossed the Atlantic on a troopship and had disembarked in Casablanca late at night. The next morning I awoke to a landscape so colorful in so many ways that I've been drawn to Moslem places — Damascus, Omdurman and Timbuktu — ever since. My fellow GIs and I were put on a train that consisted of decrepit wooden boxcars called "forty-and-eights," so named because they had been used by the French army in World War I to transport forty men or eight horses. Proof of that historical fact was still stenciled on the side of every car: QUARANTE HOMMES OU HUIT CHEVAUX.

For six days I sat in the open door of that crowded train with my legs hanging out over Morocco, Algeria and Tunisia, not wanting the trip to end. Everything was so new, so unrelated to anything I had encountered in my Protestant upbringing and my Ivy League education. Who *were* these exotic Arabs and Berbers? How did these countries get to look this

way, half Islamic, half French provincial? What was
their history? I wanted to know, but there were no
books to tell me, even when I was later stationed at a
base not far from Algiers and could visit its bookstores. I assumed that nobody had written any such
books in English. English-speaking people thought
the civilized world stopped in Europe; *I* certainly
did.

Then, one day, a package came in the mail from
my mother. It was *Fountains in the Sand*, by Norman
Douglas. A British writer had actually walked
around Tunisia and written a book about it. Not only
that; he had done it in 1912. What kind of man would
walk around Tunisia in 1912? Just from the chapter
titles — "By the Oued Baiesh," "Stones of Gafsa,"
"The Gardens of Nefta" — I knew that the book
would answer my need for a predecessor in this
unknown land, someone who could validate the ex-
citements I was feeling myself, and it did. I was
especially grateful for the exactness of its detail.
Wherever Norman Douglas went, I felt one thing for
sure: he had been there.

This is the crucial gift that all good travel writers
bestow — the sense that they were there — and as I
look at all the travel books I've acquired since that
first debarking in Casablanca I realize that every one
of those authors provided that gift, even if, as was

often the case, they weren't primarily travel writers. Many of the books are by people who are more famous for other accomplishments (*My African Journey*, by the Rt. Hon. Winston Spencer Churchill, M.P., written in 1908) or for other kinds of writing: *The Innocents Abroad*, by Mark Twain; *In the South Seas: Being an Account of Experiences and Observations in the Marquesas, Paumotus and Gilbert Islands*, by Robert Louis Stevenson; *In Morocco*, by Edith Wharton; *Etruscan Places*, by D. H. Lawrence; *The Stones of Florence*, by Mary McCarthy. Many of the books are by adventurous women — from *A Thousand Miles up the Nile*, by Amelia R. Edwards, written in 1877, to *Where Mountains Roar: A Personal Report from the Sinai and Negev Desert*, by Lesley Hazleton, written more than a century later.

Some are journeys to dead civilizations (*Pleasure of Ruins*, by Rose Macaulay). Some are journeys between points never previously linked: *From the Cape to Cairo: The First Traverse of Africa from South to North*, by Ewart S. Grogan and Arthur H. Sharp (1900). Some are vivid memoirs of an earlier life (*A House in Bali*, by Colin McPhee; *Peking Story: The Last Days of Old China*, by David Kidd). Some are rich personal odysseys (*East of Home*, by Santha Rama Rau; *In Patagonia*, by Bruce Chatwin). Some are explorers' accounts of their own exhilarating trips (*Kon-Tiki*, by

Thor Heyerdahl). Some are accounts of earlier explorers' trips—a genre raised to perfection by Alan Moorehead, especially in *The White Nile*, a book that I reread with shameless admiration. Moorehead's feat is not only to make us feel that we are with Burton, Speke, Baker and the other doughty Victorians who sought the source of the Nile, but that we are with *him* as he follows the steps of those explorers in the Sudan, Uganda, Zanzibar and Kenya.

It's all travel writing, whatever shape it takes; the form is infinitely welcoming, renewing itself every year with writers who bring fresh powers of observation to the sites they visit, making us see those places as we have never seen them before. Today some of the best of it originates as magazine journalism, especially in *Granta* and *The New Yorker*, and has considerable reportorial importance; all travel writers, even Herodotus, even Thoreau, are reporters before they are anything else. Proof of which is this book. If any one quality unites the six writers you are about to meet, it is a curiosity to find out what makes a country or a city or a town or a tribal village unique and to bring the information back.

*They Went* is an exploration of how travel writers write. The book originated as a series of talks held at The New York Public Library in the winter of 1990, the sixth in a series in which writers discussed a particular aspect of the art and craft of writing. Previous series were devoted to biography, memoir, religious writing, the political novel and writing for children—forms that took the speakers on many bold trips, but mostly to regions of the mind, the heart, the soul and the home. It was time for some serious stretching of wings.

Mark Salzman, the youngest of the writers included here, was one of the farthest travelers. Just out of Yale, he went to China for two years to teach English at Hunan Medical College in Changsha, and the book he wrote about those years, *Iron and Silk*, which was nominated for a Pulitzer Prize and has been translated into eight languages, is an enormously likable account of the men and women he taught and learned from, especially his martial arts instructor, the great Chinese master Pan Qingfu. At no point did it occur to Salzman that he was writing a travel book. "I never accumulated much travel detail," he says, "and the places I visited made very little impression on me. On the other hand, I did remember all kinds of people who I thought were interesting. So, basically, all I did in my book was to write about the people I remembered. To me, a sense of place is nothing more than a sense of people. Whether a landscape is bleak or beautiful, it doesn't mean anything to me until a person walks into it, and then what interests me is how the person behaves in that place."

Andrea Lee was also just out of college when she went with her new husband in 1978 to the Soviet Union for ten months. They lived in student housing in Moscow — two ordinary Americans living as ordinary Russians — and the book that she fashioned from that day-to-day experience, *Russian Journal*, is therefore filtered through her own eyes and ears, not through the official truth of government guides. It's a classic traveler's book: the report of someone who was there. What emerged from her stay in Russia, she says, "was basically a collection of portraits of people under pressure, a chronicle of the odd beauties, the frequent grotesque comedy and the recurrent fear and tragedy that thrive under a system of political repression." Today, only a decade later, her book is as frozen in its time frame as Evelyn Waugh's book about Ethiopia and Norman Lewis's book about Indochina.

Vivian Gornick, who began her career as a journalist for the *Village Voice* in the sixties, went to Cairo in 1971 to immerse herself for six months in the middle-class life of that city for a book called *In Search of Ali Mahmoud*. "The whole country was in an intelligent fever," she says. "I loved them for it. I thought their condition profound, and I identified with it. Instead of analyzing my subject I merged with my subject. The Egyptians and I became one. They were nervous, I was nervous. They were needy, I was needy. They were neurotic, I was neurotic." It would be fifteen years before Gornick would write another book—*Fierce Attachments*, a memoir of growing up in the Bronx that is as lean and astringent as her Egyptian book was flabby; in fact, it's one of the best "travel" books that anyone has written about New York. Now, looking back at *In Search of Ali Mahmoud*, she ponders one of the occupational hazards of the travel form: how to avoid becoming so emotionally entwined with a place that the writer ceases to be trustworthy as a reporter.

Closer to home, Ian Frazier and Calvin Trillin take America as their territory—a decision requiring a certain courage, for in choosing to deal with the obvious in our midst they relinquish all the benefits that a writer gets by just stepping off the plane in a foreign country: instant otherness. China is easier to write about than Cheyenne, Leningrad easier than Louisville. But to see Cheyenne and Louisville written about well, to see the dailiness of America brought to life with freshness and humor, is to watch one of the hardest high-wire acts in travel writing.

*Introduction*

Nobody walks that wire with more sureness and
nerve than Frazier and Trillin.

Ian Frazier's *The Great Plains* is as various and
robust as the region he writes about—a perfect
mirror of his subject. The book is alive with his
inquisitiveness about the vast center of America — its
vibrant history and successive waves of settlement—
and with his affection for the men and women who
populated it, especially the great Indian chief Crazy
Horse. "I wanted to do a profile of a place as if it were
a person," he says, recalling how he set out alone by
car to look for that personified place. "On the Great
Plains you have to get off the paved road if you want
to see where you are. I often found that the experiences I had were interesting in direct proportion to
the risks I had taken with my car."

Calvin Trillin, whose main rule for writing about
America is that you can't quote de Tocqueville,
began writing his "U.S. Journal"—a three-thou-
sand-word article from somewhere in the United
States every three weeks—for *The New Yorker* in
1969 and kept it up for fifteen years. Even then he
didn't abandon the beat, continuing to write long
narrative pieces called "American Chronicles" that
have run in the magazine ever since. That's a lot of
writing about America, and I'm sure I'm not the only

writer who has been reading it for two decades with envy and disbelief: so much legwork, so much interviewing and note taking, so much seemingly effortless organizing of information, so many facts presented with a humor that barely tugs at our sleeve as it goes by. "What I was trying to do in 'U.S. Journal,'" Trillin says, "was to write about the country without concentrating on the government and politics of the country." Although each article was ostensibly about a place, what took Trillin to that place was a specific story. "The story was told in the context of the place," he explains, "and the piece only worked if the reader learned something about the place in addition to finding out what had happened there."

Tobias Schneebaum is like nobody in my travel library — off the chart in his total submission to the societies he drops in on, deep in the jungle, primitive beyond our twentieth-century ability to imagine their life. The British solitaries like Doughty and Lawrence who lived like Arabs and wore Arab clothes at least kept their clothes on, and it's probably safe to guess that when the desert sun went down they lit up a pipe of tobacco they had brought along from Oxford Street. In Schneebaum's case, one of the many astonishments of his first and best known book, *Keep the River on Your Right*, a chronicle of several months spent in 1955 in the interior of Peru with a Stone Age tribe of cannibals called the Akamara, is that he went, like his hosts, entirely naked—no small adjustment, one might think, for someone who was born and raised in New York City. "I have a need to travel to distant corners of the world," he says. "At times a yearning comes over me, an urgency to rid myself of the vestments of civilization, to find a new kind of freedom, one not found at home. I don't know what that freedom is or what I'm searching for. I only know it as a drive within me into the unknown."

Coming from so many directions and going to so many different points of the compass, all six writers in this book are nevertheless finally talking about the same thing: who they are in relation to the place and how that affects the story they bring back. Trillin is the objective reporter, Salzman the obliging friend; when one of his martial arts teachers asks him to climb a holy mountain and burn incense for him in a temple at the summit, he does. His traveler's reward for the arduous hike is to be asked a preposterous question by a Buddhist abbot.

For the two women writers, their identity was the most important piece of baggage they took along. Vivian Gornick, hurling herself at a conservative

Arab country where women are wholly submerged, was a Jewish feminist journalist from America: four kinds of bad news. Yet she found Cairo very familiar: "For me, Cairo was New York, a bombardment of stimuli — filthy, dusty, crowded, alive and in pain, constantly reactive, always in motion. Everyone took me out, and everyone took me home. It was nonstop family life, nonstop street life, nonstop conversation. Nonstop. That's how I remember Egypt." That familiarity, Gornick says, was her downfall. "It excited and confused me, and I romanticized it. I romanticized its seeming mysteriousness. The problem was detachment: I didn't have any. I didn't even know it was something to be prized — that without detachment there can be no story."

Andrea Lee, by contrast, explains that she grew up in the sixties as part of "an affluent, extremely bookish, extremely middle-class Afro-American family in which the adults, at least, would have been horrified to hear themselves called Afro-Americans. Descended from free mulattoes from Virginia and North Carolina in whose veins English and Irish blood was mixed with Indian, my family, theoretically as American as possible, was specialized in being outsiders." From early childhood, Lee says, she felt a "sense of eternal apartness, of being both observer and participant" — an ideal angle of vision for a writer in the Soviet Union, which, at that time, "specialized in double lives. Almost everyone we met had a public persona and a radically different private one. The private persona usually had to do with some kind of cultural or political leaning unacceptable to current party wisdom or etiquette." Lee's situation was the exact opposite of Gornick's. One was an American black reared with the detachment needed to survive in white America; the other was a white woman so romantically involved with her material that she never saw it clearly.

"Nowadays," Ian Frazier says, "most places have a double existence: one in reality and another in the imagination of people. The Great Plains have had an unusually lively imaginary existence for the past two hundred years." Time is another multiple element that he says travel writers have to juggle. "More than other kinds of writing, travel writing exists in time," Frazier points out, noting that the two centuries in which the events he describes in *The Great Plains* occurred are qualitatively different from the time he inhabits as a writer going in search of those events and describing his quest. Tobias Schneebaum, trading for decorated skulls with the primitive Asmat in the interior of New Guinea, meets high-tech workmen employed by a giant conglomerate drilling for oil. He is a traveler in two worlds that are eons apart.

Yet at some point all the levels have to merge as literature. In other nonfiction forms such disjunctions of time and reality might make a disjointed book, badly out of harmony. But good travel readers have always been adept at making leaps, at reconciling the infinite varieties of experience that the world presents. Like good travel writers, they live in constant expectation of the unexpected and in pure enjoyment of it when it comes along. This sense of partnership in the writer's own enjoyment is one of the strongest bonds in any literary genre, and the six writers in this book obviously understand that bond and trust it.

These talks were tape-recorded, and in editing them for publication I worked from transcripts of the tapes, trying to preserve the voice and the rhythms and the personality of the speakers. Listen, therefore, as you read: these are travelers' tales.

IAN FRAZIER

# Carving Your Name
on the Rock

Until my book was published I didn't know it was a travel book. When I first thought of writing it I saw it as a long profile in *The New Yorker*. I wanted to do a profile of a place as if it were a person. I became very excited about this idea, and I called William Shawn, then the editor of *The New Yorker*, and explained it to him. I told him I wanted to write a six-part profile of the Great Plains. He listened to me, and there was a pause, and then he said, "Would it be funny?"

When I was working on the book I had a hard time explaining what it was about. People almost always misheard me the first time I told them the topic. Usually they thought I had said something about airplanes. Once I got that straight I'd say, "Well, it's about the history of the Great Plains, and the geography, and the people, a little about the geology, and it's about Indians, and Crazy Horse, and the buffalo, and homesteaders, and it's kind of a travelogue, kind of an essay . . ." After the book came out my publisher sent me on a promotional trip to Denver, and I went to the warehouse of a big book distributor, where I was supposed to sign some books. It was an enormous warehouse covering several acres, with stacks and stacks of books on wooden pallets in rows that extended into the distance. They took me through the stacks to my own little pile of books, and as I sat there on a carton signing three hundred or so copies, a guy who worked on the floor driving books around with a forklift truck came up to me and told me he liked my book. I said, "Thanks, I'm glad you liked it." He said, "Yeah, I really like road books." Road book. I had never heard that term before — road movies, road shows, but never road books. So that was what all the uncertainty and hemming and hawing boiled down to in the end: a road book.

To write a road book you need a road. There are lots of roads now; there didn't use to be. About 150 years ago the main roads were rivers. Travelers to the Great Plains then often went by steamboat up the Missouri River. Even explorers who went on foot tended to stick pretty close to the river valleys; I suppose the books they later wrote could be described as river books. Many of these early American travelers were European. The books they wrote sometimes had titles like *Travels in North America* or *Travels in the Interior of North America*. North America is my own favorite destination. When I think of a romantic place to go it's usually San Antonio, Texas, or Gaylord, Michigan, or Roundup, Montana, or Cape Girardeau, Missouri. And I especially like the interior of North America; the Great Plains are about as interior as you can get.

As anyone who has traveled in the interior of North America knows, to do it you need a car. Going by car has an inevitable effect on what you write. A person who traveled by steamboat or with an overland expedition usually had a lot of company. A person who travels by car usually does not. By my informal survey, the majority of cars on the road contain only one person. To a writer that might at first seem good: I'm free, I'm on my own, I've got nobody to answer to. But if you've ever rented a car you know that's not the case. Before they hand you the keys at the rental counter they deliver a sermon about insurance waivers and damage liability. A person in a rented car is not free, but on parole. And if you own the car yourself you worry about insurance rates and repair costs and whether you could replace the car if you wrecked it. These worries restrain you; they keep you in your place. That's why people love to watch car chases in movies and on TV: each time Steve McQueen's Mustang scrapes its underside on a bump at one hundred miles an hour it's a slap at the insurance agent, the loan officer. There's an ad out now with the slogan, "It's not just a car, it's your freedom." Owning a car is not freedom; *damaging* a car is freedom.

For the traveler in the interior of North America the car is a companion with its own definite itinerary. If you're timid about your car you will drive sensibly on paved roads and stay every night in a motel. We all know that it's possible to drive from here to California and stay at more or less the same motel the entire way, in a landscape where certain elements never change. This might have been an interesting experience thirty years ago when it was still new. It might be an interesting experience if you were V. S. Naipaul just arrived here from England. But basically it's a challenge to one's powers of describing the humdrum. On the Great Plains — and I'm sure in the rest of America as well — you have to get off the paved road if you want to see where you are. I often found that the experiences I had were interesting in direct proportion to the risks I had taken with my car. If you're not getting stuck occasionally, sliding off the road, knocking your outside mirrors off, bumping your oil pan, you're not doing the job. And it helps to have a vehicle you can sleep in; that way, you won't be so upset if something goes wrong and you can't get back to the settlements before dark.

The car can also have subtle effects on your research. For example, I love historic markers. I stopped to read hundreds of them along the roads on the Great Plains; some of the information in my book I found on historic markers and no place else. I liked to read about events while standing in the very spot where the events took place. I wouldn't be unhappy in a world where every object carried a plaque or a caption or a label. But when I'm driving a winding road in New Mexico, and I've just waited twenty miles and forty-five minutes to pass a cantaloupe truck, and I finally pass the truck, and then suddenly on my right there appears a historic marker — well, I'm going to think twice about pulling over. I'd hate myself later if I kept going, but I'd be unhappy right then if I stopped. I missed a bunch of historic markers that way. Driving has an urgency about it, a hypnotic quality, which on the Plains can be very powerful. If you're going down a flat, straight, empty road at sixty miles an hour and your windshield is nine-tenths sky and you feel like you're flying, you can drive four hundred miles in a trance without seeing a thing.

Another problem with cars is that they make a

mess. When you turn off the highway you are in-juring the ground you drive on. The big forces of erosion on the Plains today, in addition to wind and water, are cows and cars. (Let's not leave out dirt bikes, either.) It's a rare piece of prairie without its own rusty muffler pipe or discarded air filter. When the Plains Indians first saw automobiles they called them "skunk wagons" because of the way they smelled. A measure of the difference between an old-time Plains Indian and me is that I like the way cars smell. That engine exhaust, pumping carbon into the atmosphere — to me it smells of departure, of adven-ture. I was pretty proud of the twenty-five thousand miles I had driven on the Plains until I read (in Bill McKibben's *The End of Nature*) that in ten thousand miles of driving an average car will put a ton of carbon into the atmosphere. So my little book, 291 pages long, sent two and a half tons of carbon into the sunny skies above the Plains.

I did most of that driving when I lived in Montana; my car was a 1976 Chevy van. After I moved back to New York and my van died I rented cars when I went to the Plains. Once I rented a Chevy Corsica from Hertz at the Midland-Odessa airport in Texas and then drove up through the Panhandle and on into Kansas and Nebraska. The days were routinely a hundred degrees or more — this was August. I made use of the air conditioner. I was spinning along through the Nebraska sandhills when suddenly there was kind of a *whomph* sound, and a white cloud came out from under the hood. The cloud flew past my window, and in my rearview mirror I could see it hanging in the air behind me. I pulled over at the next gas station, in Tryon, Nebraska, and a guy there looked at the engine and told me that my air conditioner hose had melted. For some reason, in the engine of a Chevy Corsica a rubber hose to the air-conditioning unit runs directly across the top of the engine manifold; when the manifold gets really hot, the hose melts and the refrigerant escapes. That cloud I saw was twenty-eight ounces of Freon heading for the wide-open spaces. Somewhere up there in the ozone is a little hole torn by me. When I got back to the car rental and told them what had happened they gave me a ten-dollar discount.

Given these problems with the car—problems both technical and ethical, or environmental—should the writer consider some other means of getting around? Should the writer consider, say, bicycling, or walking, or traveling on horseback, or renting a private railroad car? No, of course not. First, because I don't believe you should ever do anything that's so hard that it makes your reader tired. I've read some interesting accounts of bicycling across the Plains, but they always leave me exhausted. As for walking, you would have to be out of your mind. It would take forever. In a railroad car you would essentially be in period costume, and all the interesting railroad track routes on the Plains have been torn up long ago. A traveler on horseback would be a curiosity; I find it easier to observe when I'm not being observed myself. (Actually that horseback idea does appeal to me — it might be possible to find enough small roads and free grazing to take a horse from Mexico to Canada on the Plains.) In the end I'm afraid we're stuck with the car. It's what we've got; it is of our age.

When I travel on the Plains, people sometimes ask me why I don't live there. More often they ask why I choose to live in New York City. They ask how I can stand it. For a while these questions made me feel bad — as if I must be schizophrenic. I did most of my driving on the Plains in the course of several years — summers, mostly. After I moved back to New York I continued my research here, at The New York Public Library. I suppose that decision had to do with my affection for historic markers: this library is like the historic marker for the whole country; I pulled over here and began to read. And I can say that I was as happy — and as frustrated, confused, lonely, lost, bored, exhilarated — in the main reading room of this library as I was on the Plains. I spent much of two years here reading about places I had visited. When I was driving I bought books wherever I went, and I noticed a phenomenon: I couldn't read a book about a place once I had left the place. I couldn't read a book about North Dakota when I was in New Mexico; books about the Texas Panhandle lost their interest when I was in the alkali flats of Wyoming.

But in the main reading room here I could read about anyplace. That big hall, with all those different people doing all different kinds of work, was like a harbor with draft deep enough for any ship. I would take out books on several Great Plains topics at one time, and switch back and forth between them when I got bored. Driving the Plains and reading about them both turned out to be dusty experiences. Some of the books hadn't been touched in years. They were covered with a special kind of gray, spectral book dust made of the tiniest particles. And the old moldy smell! I read an early edition of *The Journals of Lewis and Clark* and 171-year-old chips of paper from the corners of the pages fell into my lap. I read books so old the *s*'s were *f*'s. That can really drive you crazy, by the way.

I think spending so many hours sitting in that room affected my writing, just as sitting in a car did. For example, it's hard to eat when you're working in the library. You're not allowed to eat in any of the reading rooms, and I think that's a good rule. The only problem is, if you're working in the library from ten in the morning to eight-thirty at night you get hungry. You don't want to leave your books and notes all spread out on the table, but it's a pain to pack everything up and go out to lunch; bringing a sandwich and eating out front isn't very satisfactory either. I'm sure there is a practical solution to this problem, but my own solution sometimes was just to forget about eating and work straight through. As I was sitting there reading about what old plainsmen ate — how the Lewis and Clark expedition once had nothing for dinner but a crow; how the Stephen Long expedition of 1819 ate a heron; how the Snake Indians made a paste of ants and then made soup of the paste; how a traveler named Duke Paul of Württemberg had a meal of turtle eggs and bear meat on a sandspit in the Missouri River; how the Comanche liked to eat curdled buffalo milk from the stomach of a freshly killed buffalo calf; how breakfast for passengers on a Montana stagecoach line consisted of "good hot coffee and venison steaks and flapjacks" — my mouth would water. Raw buffalo liver sprinkled with gall and a few grains of gunpowder began to sound delicious. I began to keep track of these foods in a special section in my notes, and eventually a lot of that section ended up in the book.

Reading about places where I had been, I saw them again more clearly. Reading Indian agent James McLaughlin's account — in his book *My Friend the Indian* — of the morning he sent police to Sitting Bull's camp to arrest Sitting Bull, I remembered the site of the camp, and the way the prairie grasses grew, and the gully that led down to the river bottom, and the buckskin-colored water of the Grand River flowing nearby, and the rolling prairie in the distance that the police must have crossed. Reading about the awful mess left behind on the Custer battlefield — the cartridges, lanyards, swivel clips, guns, corpses, folding money, the cavalry boot with a foot still in it — I remembered how the land rolls on that battlefield, how a person standing down in a dip can be totally hidden from a person standing in another dip forty feet away. Reading a good scholarly article about Billy the Kid's first arrest — for stealing clothes from a Chinese laundry in Silver City, New Mexico, when he was fifteen — and his subsequent escape by climbing up a jail-house chimney, I remembered how little those old New Mexican towns are, and how close together the adobe houses, and how narrow the streets that Billy the Kid shot people on. After I had read about places I often went back and looked at them again. It was a process of reading and looking and reading again.

Nowadays most places have a double existence: one in reality, in their physical selves, and another in the imaginations of people. The Great Plains have had an unusually lively imaginary existence for the past two hundred years or so. The record of that existence is here in The New York Public Library. The imaginary existence has intruded violently and often into the simple physical existence. To give an example: after the Plains were cleared of buffalo — "shot out," in the buffalo hunters' term — entre-preneurs immediately brought in cattle to take ad-vantage of all that empty grazing land. The herds quickly increased until there were more cattle than the range could hold. In the winter of 1886–87 a blizzard came down from Canada and killed hun-dreds of thousands of cattle. The event is sometimes called "the big die-up." It wiped out investors in Chicago, New York, London, Edinburgh. Very likely, many of those investors had been persuaded to put their money in Great Plains ranches by a book that came out in 1881 called *The Beef Bonanza; or, How to Get Rich on the Plains*, by General James S. Brisbin. I found a first edition of it here in the Library.

History has made it a comical book. Much of the

book is figures, which begin with a sum—say, $500—and go on and on through columns until several pages later your original $500 has become $10,000. The copy I read here had ancient underlining and marginal notes in a cute, hopeful nineteenth-century hand. I remember one sentence to the effect that an initial investment in cattle would grow to whatever enormous amount within five years while paying an annual interest of ten percent the entire time. That sentence was underlined twice. The poor guy. Get-rich-quick books have always been around, but this one had the advantage of a few years of actual prosperity in the cattle business to make it seem halfway credible. The effect of the big die-up on the landscape was certainly real: dead cattle filled the ravines, the spring thaw stank, the prairies were emptied once again, and the open range gave way to barbed-wire fences everywhere. But the real agent of this change in the landscape—the virus of hope that caused it—is in the pages of this book.

When you drive on the Great Plains, sometimes it's hard to understand why the land is so empty, why the small towns are dying, why you get so bored. And it's hard to write about the boredom without being boring. The boredom is important, however: I don't believe you know a place until you've been really bored in it. When you read about the Great

Plains in the library, when you follow its fantasy existence in the mind of this country for more than two hundred years, you see that our imagination as a society has never been equal to the challenge of living there. We've had one wrong idea after the next about the Plains.

First we called them the Great American Desert, when early explorers happened to go west through the sandhills along the Arkansas and the Platte rivers and extended those sandhills indefinitely north and south in their minds. The Great Plains are not a desert. Then the Plains were the Wild West, and people went there in search of an adventurous life which their very presence caused to disappear. Thousands of buffalo hunters made millions of dollars hunting themselves out of a job. Then the Plains became the Cattle Kingdom; that lasted a few years. All these eras were like spasms.

Then came the homesteader boom. The railroads sold the Plains as a garden spot, "the Garden in the Grasslands." Books I read about this period contained reproductions of railroad circulars, which always told prospective homesteaders not to come if they were afraid of hard work. The homesteaders went and worked harder than most of us can even imagine. Husbands and wives aged in a few seasons, spent their youth, went broke and left, thinking they must not have worked hard enough. The Great Plains are not a garden; you can't make a living there on a 160-acre homestead. Then World War I came along and the Plains were supposed to win the war with wheat. Farmers plowed from hedgerow to hedgerow. The war ended, the sod cover was gone from the prairie, drought hit, the wind blew, and suddenly the Great Plains were the Dust Bowl. During the energy crisis of fifteen years ago, people were drilling and digging the Plains, which by then had become part of the New Energy Frontier.

Last summer two professors from Rutgers University came up with another idea of what to do with the Great Plains. They reasoned that since population was leaving the Plains and agriculture was failing, we should consider restoring the Plains to their pre-agricultural state and bring back the buffalo. Their name for this restored version of the Great Plains is the Buffalo Common. When I first heard this name it tickled me; I was pleased to see that the Plains hadn't lost their knack for inspiring ambitious management schemes with catchy labels. The Buffalo Common seemed a worthy successor to the Great American Desert or the Garden in the Grasslands. It would be nice if someone could buy up a lot of marginal rangeland on the Plains, with a healthy watershed and some flowing creeks and good bottomland, and

restore the prairie grasses and the buffalo and ante-
lope and elk, and then turn the place into a park. I'm
sure that the tens or hundreds of thousands of black-
powder enthusiasts and historical re-creationists in
this country would want to go there; I'd want to go
there myself. But then I read an article about the
Buffalo Common that the two Rutgers professors
wrote for the *Washington Post*. They mentioned that
their plan would spare "viable" urban centers such as
Cheyenne, Wyoming, and Bismarck, North Dakota.
What these professors envision is not some relatively
small park, but buffalo running around everywhere
from Texas to Canada. What a remarkable, nutty
idea.

Public discussion about the Buffalo Common is a
development that has occurred since my book was
published. There have been other developments: a
man I traveled with and wrote about has died; energy
exploration on the Plains has slowed; certain parts of
the Plains were so dry last summer that there was talk
of another Dust Bowl. More than other kinds of
writing, travel writing exists in time. To begin with,
there is the time the journey or journeys involved
took to complete. Then there is the time — the year
or years — in which the travel took place. As I said
earlier, history made General Brisbin's book about

how to get rich on the Plains comical. At the end of my book I compare the Great Plains to the steppes of Russia, and I discuss the Minuteman and MX missiles in underground silos scattered across the Plains. I describe the Great Plains as a weapons system that is aimed at Russia. Recent events have aged that observation. If events continue on their present course that observation may age to the point of quaintness. Travel writing is perishable. I find that when I'm reading a book of bygone travels I become irritated with curiosity about what the place is like today — can you still swim in the river, as the writer did? Can you still eat the fish? Are the houses still roofed with thatch? This problem has to do not only with travel writing but with all nonfiction. If you look in the Classics or Literature section of any bookstore you'll see mainly works of fiction. Nonfiction is about the physical world, and over time the physical world tends to disappear.

Not only do the places change that the traveler visits; the time that the journey requires also changes. A traveler today has a sense of time completely different from that of a traveler a hundred years ago. Journeys used to be measured in weeks or months: it was a five weeks' voyage from Bristol, England, to New York; it was a journey of a week or more from New York to Pittsburgh; it took four or five weeks to cross the prairies from the Missouri River to the Rocky Mountains. Today it's forty-five minutes by plane from here to Pittsburgh, three and a half hours to the Rocky Mountains. Most journeys in America today take minutes or hours. There are no two places within the lower forty-eight states more than a day's travel apart, given favorable circumstances. In former times, when a traveler set out on a journey he was pretty much stuck with it. Marco Polo couldn't say, "Hey, I've got a free weekend here in Peking, think I'll jet home and check on the wife." Lewis and Clark couldn't say, "It's not much fun here in the Rocky Mountains, let's chopper back to St. Louis and then pick up again where we left off." Today, if a person gets tired of a journey he can simply go home on the next plane.

Because of this, a traveler nowadays doesn't have a simple, ready-made structure waiting for him when he sits down to describe his journey. He can't as easily begin his book at place A and proceed through places B through Z, ending up back at A. When he gets to place F the reader wonders — at least *I* wonder — why he doesn't take a break and go back to A for a while. Maybe I'm the only person who is bothered by this. It's just that I have trouble with books that go in a straight line, when our world has so many ricochets in it, so many bounces and bends and turns. A modern travel book that begins at point A and proceeds through point Z seems to me as corny and antique as a modern novel that begins, "Chapter One: I Am Born." Sometimes I'm reading a book and the author is in some exotic place and he's keeping the exotic atmosphere perking along and I know for a fact that someplace along in there the guy called his accountant back in the city and had a three-hour conversation about his Keogh plan. Or that at some point he went to a Holiday Inn and watched MTV and was nowhere at all for sixteen hours. I guess I know that because I did that kind of thing myself. I'm not saying a writer should always put that stuff in — should yank the reader back to his armchair from the Shangri-la he has transported him to. But I think the writer should at least consider it.

One reason the writer can give for including himself — his state of mind, incidentals of his life — in a piece of travel writing is that places tend to look the way you feel when you look at them. More than that, if enough people over time feel the same way in a particular place, the place will start to sympathize and will reflect those feelings in its physical appearance. So many people have gotten divorced in Reno, Nevada, that now Reno looks a bit the way people feel when they've gotten divorced. Greyhound bus stations look the way people feel when they're riding on Greyhound buses. No matter how hospitals try to cheer up waiting rooms, they still look like the misery people feel there. In southwestern Wyoming there's a mountain called Laramie Peak. It was the first glimpse that pioneers coming up the Platte River road, later the Oregon Trail, had of the Rockies. For some travelers it was the first mountain they had ever seen. So many people looked at Laramie Peak with hope that it still looks that way today—like Ararat, like a promise, like hope realized. When a writer observes a place he is contributing to how that place looks.

Travelers who went west on the Oregon Trail in the 1840s and 1850s took a growing season—spring, summer, fall—to get from the East to their new homes in Oregon and California. About thirty-four thousand of them died between the last settlements in the East and the settlements on the West Coast. It was an average of about seventeen deaths per mile of the trail. Most of the emigrants walked most of the way. Their feet wore grooves in rock. When they got to a campsite on the Laramie River in what is now Wyoming, they generally rested for a few days. Near that campsite is a big sandstone outcropping called Register Cliff. While the travelers waited to go on, many of them carved their names on the rock. It was a big event—you can see it by the care they took in their carving. Some were people who had clearly spent hours and hours of childhood practicing the evenly rounded letters of cursive handwriting. The names they left behind, some of them, are so elegant — so enlivened with serifs and fancy underlinings — that they can hardly be called graffiti. Today Register Cliff is a state park, consisting of the cliff, a parking lot and a restroom. The older names on the cliff are protected by a chain-link fence. Modern names have spread all over the unprotected parts of the cliff like a rash. Clearly, a person who races up to Register Cliff in a car and carves his name and races away doesn't have the same concentration as a person who arrived there after weeks of travel by wagon train. I remember "Edna + Kenny 1979" and "Nat 'n Pat 1977."

It takes effort for me not to see the more recent names on the rock as ugly and awful. But my handwriting is no prize, either. I'm sure that if I carved my name on the rock I would appear to people of the future as a true member of the "Nat 'n Pat" era and not a member of the age of the pioneers. What the travel writer is doing, in essence, is carving his name on the rock. He is saying, "I passed this way too." If I carved my name on the rock I would say to myself, "Yes, I came here by car, which pollutes the environment. No, I have no idea what it would be like to come here by wagon when this was wilderness. Yes, I will be gone in a matter of minutes. Yes, I am distracted by thoughts of what I'm going to eat and what I'm going to buy and watch on TV and spend and earn. No, I can't imagine the coherence of the culture that produced such beautiful handwriting. But I think I'd like to try to do a little carving anyway, and I hope it turns out pretty."

———

*The following excerpts from the question-and-answer period raised further points about the writing experience.*

*Q. With an undertaking like* The Great Plains *you obviously had all kinds of personal experiences and tons of research material. Can you tell us about the process whereby you take this vastness and reduce it to something manageable?*

*A.* In the case of personal experiences the choice is relatively easy. You have so many experiences that you just pick the best ones, because readers are going to get tired of the less interesting ones. Of course, what you're really writing about is yourself — *The Great Plains* is an internal landscape, a memoir. On the other hand, a book called *The Great Plains* had better be about the Great Plains, so you find ways to write about yourself within that framework.

As for the historical and travel material, I now think I narrowed it down more than I needed to. I originally wrote these pieces for *The New Yorker*, and I was aware that people in New York say things like "Nebraska is the most boring place I've ever been in my life" and "I looked out the airplane window and there was nothing down there." I didn't want readers to say, "He's right, it *is* boring." I once saw a funny map of the United States that had things like NU-CLEAR WASTE ZONE for New Jersey, and in the middle of the country it had a big gray section labeled BOREDOM ZONE. I compared it with an old map of mine, and the Boredom Zone is in the exact spot where the maps used to say Great American Desert. So I was very selective about using material that I hoped wouldn't be boring. But after the book came out I found that people's tolerance — what they thought was interesting — was much greater than I had imagined. I could have included considerably more material.

When I first learned reporting, another reporter on *The New Yorker* showed me his notebooks. His method was to just go through his notes and circle his favorite things in red and then make his piece out of the things that were circled. So that's essentially what I did in this book. I just took my favorite things — the things I like to talk about most — and found a way to put them all together. The things you like tend to have a symmetry with each other. It's similar to what happens when you invite all the people you like to a party; you realize that each person is some part of your personality.

*Q. I grew up in Minnesota and went to school in Montana, so when I moved here to New York City it was very scary. Did you feel a sense of relief when you went out west and saw all this calmness?*

A. Not at all. When I was first in Big Fork, Montana, I was scared of the blond people. I've never seen so many blond people. Actually I had expected to feel relief; my fantasy in New York was that I had been living in some kind of behavioral sink and now I was going out to God's country and it was going to be great. But I found that whatever is wrong in New York, the virus is nationwide. I was really scared many times out there. In one place I had some neighbors who were terrifying. They would say things like, "There's a nest of devil worshipers in this town," and I thought, "There isn't a psychiatrist for fifty miles." I remember calling someone at *The New Yorker*, and he was going on about how horrible New York was. I told him, "New York is an island of light."

*Q. In your book you go far back in the history of the Great Plains and you describe many different ideas that people have had about what was going to happen there. Did you find any common thread leading to some notion about what the Great Plains are likely to become in the future?*

A. Unfortunately, the common thread across two hundred years is exploitation. Whether I was writing about the killing of the buffalo, or the cattle kings, or the homesteaders, it was always basically a way of taking the cream off this place. But I feel that the Plains may have all kinds of uses that nobody has yet dreamed of. I think that as the world gets more crowded there will be more and more people who will want to go to a bank where you don't have to stand in line, or where there is plenty of parking. There *is* plenty of parking. I also think that there are now enough white people who have lived on the Great Plains long enough so that there's a pretty good coalition between Native Americans and ranchers and other old settlers. These people understand that this is a land that you can't finally bend to your own wishes. The lesson of the Great Plains is that it's a place that does what it wants.

ANDREA LEE

# Double Lives

Ten years ago, when I was just out of college, I spent a year living in the Soviet Union and wrote a book, *Russian Journal*, about the people I met and the places I saw. Given what has happened in Eastern Europe since then, I might as well have written a book about dynastic Egypt, or about Beirut in its palmy days as "little Paris." The Russia I came to know was Brezhnev's empire on the eve of the years of decline of economy and morale that arrived with the eighties; the atmosphere was one of conscious stagnation and unbearable cynicism. In the university dormitory where I lived, propaganda posters were starting to gear up for communist empire-building in Afghanistan and Angola, and the friends I made — whether students, workers or intellectuals — talked with despairing nihilism about a Russia whose corruption and deep injustices would remain unchanged until they were destroyed in the cataclysm of World War III.

I believed what they believed, and the book that emerged from my sojourn in the Soviet Union was basically a collection of portraits of people under pressure, a chronicle of the odd beauties, the frequent grotesque comedy and the recurrent fear and tragedy that thrive under a system of political repression. The dawn of glasnost established my belief in miracles and, happily, turned my book into a period piece. When I look at it now I think of one of those frozen mammoths they dug out of the tundra — not that the prose is stiff and archaic, but the whole thing belongs to an epoch that has vanished.

Any number of people more qualified than I are talking and writing about the drama of Eastern Europe these days, and I'm not here to add one more set of observations. What I want to talk about is that past Russia that's frozen in my *Russian Journal* — the Russia that was a watershed in my career as a writer, inspiring a first book that was written with passion and a sense of personal investment. I want to talk about some of the forces that drew one writer into such intimate contact with a culture theoretically alien to her own.

The situation that impelled me to write *Russian Journal* was that I took part in a scholarly exchange between the United States and the Soviet Union, accompanying my husband, a Harvard student completing a dissertation in Russian history, during his stay at Moscow State University. The journal form of the book was suggested by William Shawn, then the editor of *The New Yorker*, who encouraged me to write a "Reporter at Large" piece for the magazine. But there was a deeper logic to the creation of the book, which I saw only much later.

In Russia I adopted the habit of scribbling observations on every available scrap of paper. On the back of a November Seventh card that someone had sent me I dashed off this rather naive and high-handed entry: "European and European-American artists have so often been drawn to the exoticism of darker-skinned, simpler cultures in warmer climates. The exposure to something so clearly defined as alien, as the furthest limits of 'other,' gives a jolt of energy that propels inspiration many steps along. It's logical that an artist should feel like a foreigner. As for me, a writer with mixed African and European blood, I find that I am interested in primitivism but uninterested in Africa or the warm countries. My own impulse toward what is alien has attracted me instead to an exotic northern country of white-skinned barbarians."

This is the kind of observation one usually, thank goodness, keeps to oneself and feels really embarrassed about ten years later. But it's interesting because it points out the fact that, for me, Russia all my life represented an instinctive goal—the farthest possible psychological and cultural distance from home. And like all such goals, its nature was determined long beforehand by the earliest circumstances of my life.

I grew up in the sixties, in the suburbs of Philadelphia, part of an affluent, extremely bookish, extremely middle-class Afro-American family, in which the adults, at least, would have been horrified to hear themselves called Afro-Americans. Descended from free mulattoes from Virginia and North Carolina in whose veins English and Irish blood was mixed with Indian, my family, theoretically as American as possible, was specialized in being outsiders. My parents, a minister and a teacher, were deeply involved in the civil rights struggle and yet also clearly felt apart—they certainly lived apart—from the poorer, blacker masses with whom they were declaring solidarity. At the same time, having grown up under de facto segregated conditions in the North, they had a basic deep suspicion and distrust of the mainstream white American society they were trying to integrate.

Throughout our childhood, my two brothers and I often found ourselves in the position of integrating something or other, whether it was schools, camps or neighborhood friends. We grew adept at assimilation without absorption, at double lives, and developed an esprit de corps of a tiny garrison of spies: we went everywhere and belonged nowhere. In a racially divided society — and for all our parents' dreams, America in the sixties and seventies continued to draw the line — we moved on two sides, with double knowledge and double insecurity.

From earliest childhood I carried an assumption in my bones that I would travel widely and live in countries far away from where I was born. It was an assumption that did not grow from what Baudelaire called "the great malady: horror of one's home." It was not based on a sense of escaping the United States or my life there, but rather on an instinct for following an innate bent, or talent, for being a foreigner somewhere. This bent tied in neatly with — or perhaps even was the source of — a tendency I began to discover in myself at the age of four or five: to observe the world around me and write down things about it, or to invent things even more fantastic than what I had observed. As early as I can remember, I had starred in an ongoing interior adventure novel. Composing and writing stories, I had discovered, went well with my sense of eternal apartness, of being both observer and participant. I didn't write from a sense of wanting to escape into fantasy or to escape an unhappy reality so much as to make a natural response to a natural inclination. A desire to travel, reduced to its essence, usually means a desire to understand more about the world, and the impulse to write is really the same thing.

All these feelings connected themselves with Russia. I was privately a rebellious little girl, with an abiding sense of being contrary to prevailing opinions. As such I imagined, as did a lot of other children in cold war America, that if the established wisdom floating in the air, diffused by television and *Life* magazine, said that the Soviet Union was hell, then it must be, if not exactly heaven, something perilously attractive, something alluring, like a book hidden under sweaters in a drawer in a parent's bedroom. I had a highly colored vision of Russia as a combination of a sort of satanic cult, churning out colossal war machines, and a dark fantasyland of birch trees, steppes, troikas, onion domes and matryoshka dolls.

In my imagination I endowed Russians with fascinating saturnine qualities and pined to meet one. I listened to recordings of Tchaikovsky, Stravinsky and Borodin and devoured fairy tales about Baba Yaga, the Russian witch, and her house on chicken legs. Russia never quite became a mania but was always a sane, sustained interest. Fortunately for me, my elementary school, a private one run by the Society of Friends, encouraged in us an apolitical interest in the culture of the Soviet Union, at a time when Khrushchev was widely considered the antichrist. At my sixth-grade graduation I gave a short memorized talk on the contributions of Russia to the art world.

The attraction held through high school and college, where I developed a passion for Russian literature, especially Tolstoy and Pasternak, and although I didn't choose to marry the young man who became my husband because he was a student of Russian history, it certainly didn't displease me. It seemed, in fact, that I had been expecting it all my life.

Despite all this pent-up enthusiasm, my first few days in the Soviet Union were a shock. I spent most of the time in tears. The first impression I had of life in Russia was pressure, consistent, strong and unvarying from all sides, as if I had suddenly descended thousands of feet under the ocean. Passes and docu-

ments, innumerable lists of things that were forbidden at certain times of the day or forbidden to all
eternity, the red propaganda posters blazing out from
the university corridors and the tops of buildings, the
physical hardship of life, the difficulty of finding an
edible meal at the university cafeteria, the packed
buses, the long lines and empty shelves in the
stores—all suggested to me that in this country
human life was reduced to a minimum level of sur-
vival and little else. I felt that under such pressure
individual lives had to be squashed into strange
shapes, and I was right.

But those shapes, when I began to make friends
and get to know people, were not as unfamiliar as I
anticipated. On our first night in Moscow my husband and I met a student our own age who turned out
to be the grandson of the Soviet political leader
Vyacheslav Molotov. "Slava" formed part of the
official greeting committee for American exchange
students at the Moscow airport, where we had been
confronted by a Byzantine bureaucracy and masses
of peasants with shawled heads. Slava stood out
immediately, relaxed and casually elegant in a pair of
jeans and a tweed jacket that would have made him
indistinguishable at a seminar at any Ivy League
college. Listening to him give cryptic, modest replies
to questions about where and how he lived, observ-

ing his clear discomfort when confronted with peasants, I realized not only that I had come into contact with my first member of the Soviet elite, but that here was someone leading the kind of double life that I was familiar with.

As I was to discover, the Soviet Union at that time specialized in double lives. Almost everyone we met had a public persona and a radically different private one. Obviously the private persona usually had to do with some kind of cultural or political leaning unacceptable to current party wisdom or etiquette. Staunch young communist leaders who spent hours in university Komsomol meetings condemning every facet of the bourgeois West spent their free time obsessively compiling vast collections of disco music. A stalwart taxi driver who had lived through the Leningrad blockade and professed to despise effete capitalists might confess late at night that he had read three Harold Robbins novels. Physics professors played clandestine jazz; the sweet, wholesome exemplars of Soviet womanhood who acted as guides and watchdogs for foreign tourists spent their lives scheming to get their hands on jean skirts and sets of Western underwear.

Everyone had something to hide — even, and probably especially, the authorities — and it was also rumored that many of the flamboyant nonconformist artists and dissidents we students came in contact with had double lives as well, as informers. Two of our best friends that year were brothers from Leningrad who took the kind of cynical pleasure in their double lives that seemed to be the token of the Brezhnev years. Both were Komsomol leaders and top students with solid careers in the *apparat* ahead of them; for them, unconventional behavior or over-fraternizing with foreigners could have been disastrous. Yet each one took a manic delight in dressing up in black-market clothes and going out and pretending to be visiting Westerners. In this guise they would even pick up naive Russian girls. They called this risky game "passing," a term that sent a shiver of recognition down my spine, given my own experience with the stereotypes and traditions of black America. In fact, thinking of those brothers, I jotted down on yet another scrap of paper one day: "The degree of dissatisfaction and self-loathing I see in the two of them, as well as the sense of belonging neither in one world or another, are all too familiar to me. The psychological effects of a totalitarian system and of racism in a democratic country have a certain amount of overlap."

Because of the way I look, most Russians tended to assume that I was that not-unusual phenomenon, a

Cuban exchange student, and so I didn't attract much attention as I tramped around in a sheepskin coat, my hands full of net bags bulging with cheese and black bread. And that was just the way I wanted it. I didn't want to have an impact on Russia; I wanted to perceive it in a state as close as possible to the way it might have been if I hadn't been there. When I started on the first entries for the "Reporter at Large" journal I wanted to do for *The New Yorker*, I felt that my first ambition would be to a create a window pane through which everything I was seeing would come through to other people.

The entries came easily, mainly because of a combination of circumstances that, for me at least, were ideal. First was this sense of instinctive understanding of, and familiarity with, the double lives I found there. Yet there was also the untold stimulation of being somewhere so very far away from everywhere I had known — to have reached, finally, a place that had always represented strangeness, otherness and romantic rebellion to me. Beyond that was the fact that I was newly married, and Russia, this strange new daily life, seemed part and parcel of the new estate, the emotional adventure that I had embarked on. My husband, who had loved and studied Russia for seven years, inspired me with daring, with a greed for knowledge of the country he loved. Occasionally we took this sentiment a bit too far, as we did in Yerevan, Armenia. There we unwisely struck up a friendship over vodka with a local gangster chief who ended the evening by threatening our lives if my husband didn't accept his generous offer to buy me.

We used to go out carousing every night with Soviet friends, talking till dawn and throwing empty vodka bottles out of windows. In the morning I would totter in, hung over, to the Lenin Library near Red Square and write down with violent immediacy descriptions of people I had met, what we had discussed, and how Russia smelled and tasted. The reading room of the library was an extremely deluxe one, mainly reserved for the upper crust of distinguished Soviet scholars, all of whom seemed to be over eighty. The room was grudgingly opened through some quirk of the exchange program, to us Americans in our twenties, who gossiped like boarding school kids and sneaked in smelly sandwiches of black bread and sausage and thermoses of tea.

I would sip that black Russian tea, oversweetened with honey from the peasant market, and, staring occasionally at the snow falling over the gold domes of the Kremlin churches, would submerge myself in Russian literature, especially Turgenev and Pasternak. In that library, it seemed as if I almost memorized *Dr. Zhivago* and Turgenev's *Sportsman's*

*Sketches,* both of which had the kind of condensed, episodic narrative that I was striving for. Then I would turn to my own work, which looked like poor stuff beside the masters, but which came tumbling out faster and faster, like the snow outside. Rarely since then have I felt that my writing was so direct a response to experience, as if life lived were an inhalation, and the work an exhalation.

Around us, other exchange students became directly and desperately entangled in Russian life, usually by falling in love. There were many improbable romances, and not solely for the convenience of getting an exit visa for a Russian spouse. I was witness at the wedding of a British law student, a cultivated and sensible young woman, and a cheerful, seven-foot Soviet circus performer. Another of my friends, a quintessentially laid-back Californian, a graduate student at UCLA, fell desperately in love with a Tartar girl, celebrated his marriage to her in a lavish blowout at the Intourist hotel and disappeared with her, presumably to spend the rest of his days in the bosom of her vast extended family in Kazan. Others fell in love with poets, dissident artists or rapacious Soviet beauties, who saw in the homeliest, most unprepossessing exchange students a ticket to the paradise of the West. I think it was fortunate for me that I was so recently and happily married that I didn't plunge into the Soviet experience to the point at which emotion might have obliterated my powers of observation. As it was, I was able to feel passionately about the country — hating the constant presence of repression large and small, and loving the people I met — and to maintain enough objectivity to write about it.

So, sitting in the Lenin Library, I was impelled to write by a sense of being at the farthest possible point from my home, from what I knew, in a country that to me had always represented the extreme of otherness to which I, as a rebel, needed to go. At the same time I experienced an extraordinary sense of comprehension and familiarity as I watched the adjustment of the people around me to the intense pressure of daily life. So very familiar did I find this mixture, in fact, that between stints of writing the entries of *Russian Journal* I was inspired to begin work on a collection of autobiographical short stories about my childhood and my college days, a collection that in a few years' time was to become my first novel, *Sarah Phillips*. The theme of the stories was social pressure, alienation and double lives, and although at the time I saw writing about myself as a respite from writing about Russia, I now see *Russian Journal* and *Sarah Phillips* as a diptych, complementary variations on the same theme. I had previously tried for several years to write about my childhood, but only in Russia did my book begin to coalesce.

My feeling that I should efface myself as much as possible in *Russian Journal* and let the country come through was perhaps strengthened by the circumstance that I was at the same time working on a book that was emphatically about myself. As my year in the Soviet Union went on and I got deeper into writing about Russia, I consciously decided not to add any autobiographical explanation to the book, to mention my background only once, and then to let it go. I adopted this policy partly as a tease and partly with the quite serious idea that any book of the kind written by someone describing herself as a black American would be viewed by some myopic literary people as "a black look at Russia." In fact, I was justified in this view by some of the silly comments made in reviews and during interviews after the book came out. A reviewer for the *New York Times* suggested that I had cheated the reader by withholding a valuable part of my Russian experience— presumably the dumbfounded reaction of Russians who had never seen a person of African descent. A television reviewer in Cleveland asked me how I had gotten along without soul food for a year in the Soviet Union. These and other comments were valuable to me in that they reminded me just how flat and limited the American idea of a black person is and, therefore, of the nature of the pressure I had grown up with — the pressure which, though infinitely milder, was related to what I had seen in the Soviet Union.

Many of the friends I made in Russia and wrote about in *Russian Journal* emigrated to the West even before Gorbachev hove into view. The two Komsomol brothers married Finnish girls and got themselves transferred to Helsinki, where both had to work as Russian teachers before being able to continue their studies in linguistics and engineering. A few anti-establishment artists I knew immigrated to the United States and made a success in the bustling world of emigré art. A young female writer I had known well went to California and, in the time-honored American tradition, promptly sued me for including her in my book. A young engineering student I taught English to moved to Austin, Texas, went to the university and became a dentist. Every one of the emigré friends I talked to have had attacks of intense yearning for the Soviet Union, the country they had hardly been able to wait to leave. One by one they confided to me their difficulties with getting along in a country in which so much is permitted, in which so much responsibility rests on the individual. Some were outraged by the crime and disorder of the

United States; others felt paralyzed by the degree of choice they suddenly had.

I understood them very well, because I myself had a fraction of the same feeling when I returned to the West after a year in Russia, the same disorientation following a year of repression. For me it was obviously a different situation: I was going home, following on the heels of the manuscript of *Russian Journal* as it sped by diplomatic pouch to New York, and the Russians had just arrived in a country that represented everything contrary to what they had grown up with. Yet although I could never experience the feeling on that same level, I could glimpse and imagine what they were feeling. It was this kind of glimpse, this momentary flash of understanding, that had always made traveling worthwhile to me — seeing oneself, for a second's flash, in another person, and comprehending that person. Similarly, I can understand the heady sense of triumph, the giddy disorientation, that Russians who chose to stay in the Soviet Union are now feeling under Gorbachev.

My former English student, the one who became a dentist in Austin, confided to me recently that when he moved into his first American apartment, in Brighton Beach, in Brooklyn, he had lined a closet with photographs and drawings from the Soviet Union and installed a bright light in it. Then he would lead his American acquaintances and friends in there and close the door on them. "I just wanted them to get a look," he said. "Just pure looking, without judging too much, is the best way to understand."

That, without realizing it, is what I was going after in *Russian Journal*. If you ask what it takes to convey a sense of place, I would say that it's best to draw on whatever passion and empathy you can, based on your own experience, and then step back and stay out of the picture.

MARK SALZMAN

*Peopling the*
*Landscape*

I once had a college English teacher who said that the most important element in travel writing was "a strong sense of place." She assigned us to go visit an unfamiliar place and write about it. I chose the woods behind the Yale Bowl and described the rocks, trees and moss as "strongly" as I could. I was bored stiff by the assignment and wondered why anyone would waste his time describing a place when we have photographs to do that for us. At that time I thought travel books were tourist diaries written by people who had nothing better to do than wander around poor countries and gush about the friendly natives, the quaint architecture and the fresh bread.

Then, several years later, I ended up teaching English at a medical college in China and wrote a book about it called *Iron and Silk*. To my surprise, I started finding my book in the Travel section of bookstores. At first I didn't attach much significance to that because I also found it under Social Sciences, Biography, History, Sports: Martial Arts, and Eastern Mysticism. But when I was invited to give one of the talks in this series I began to rethink my definition of travel writing.

I didn't go to China with the intention of traveling around the country and then writing about it. I had grown up with an interest in China from watching kung fu movies when I was a teenager — the kind where enlightened monks do back handsprings and then pause in midair just long enough to plant a spear in the forehead of an evil warlord. That sort of thing appealed to me, so I started studying martial arts. Later, when I went to Yale, I learned to speak and read and write Chinese, hoping that Chinese philosophy would improve me. Unfortunately, reading Chinese philosophy in the original didn't improve me any more than reading it in translation had. I remember opening the *Tao Te Ching*, a classic philosophical text, and being able to read in classical Chinese: "The world originates in Being. And Being originates in Non-being." And nothing happened — no brilliant insights, no oneness with the universe, no peace of mind. Meanwhile all my friends were getting high-paying starting positions at investment banks. (They're in jail now, but at the time I was very jealous.)

Toward the end of my senior year I signed up for a job teaching English in Hunan. I had never thought about actually going to China, because my interest had always been in traditional Chinese art and philosophy, not in socialist reconstruction. But since I had learned the language and was no longer using it to read books about Being and Non-being, I thought I should give China a try. I also hoped that I could study with a martial arts teacher in China, but I didn't count on it because I had been told that Chinese teachers were very conservative — they wouldn't teach a foreigner because foreigners are lazy and decadent. Well, we know that's pretty much true, but I didn't want *them* to know it, so when I got to Hunan I pretended to be very upright and disciplined. I got up early every morning and did push-ups and hoped that one of the teachers would see me. And eventually one of them did.

At the end of two years I went back home and I still didn't have any idea what I wanted to do with my life. I wasn't qualified for anything. My only job offer came from an uncle in Chicago who is a contractor. He paves roads, and he was interested in having me translate for his company — they wanted to pave

China. But somehow that didn't appeal to me. Then one day a friend of mine said, "You ought to write about your martial arts teacher, the 'Iron Fist.' You're always talking about him, and it would make a great little short story." So I said O.K., and I went and wrote the story, and my friend liked it. He said he had a friend in New York who had just started a job in either publishing or banking—he couldn't remember which—and he asked if he could send the story to her. Luckily, it turned out to be publishing, and a few weeks later she called and asked if I had any more stories about my experiences in China.

I said yes and went off and wrote another one and sent it to her. She called back and said, "Actually, I'd like to see them all at once." I said, "No, I'd rather have you see them one at a time." So I wrote some more stories, and after I had sent her about eight she took the plunge and went before her publishing committee and they agreed to go ahead with the book. So I spent the spring and summer writing the rest of it, and by fall it was done.

Now at no time did I think what I was doing was travel writing. I had gone to one place in China and lived there for two years and come home; I never accumulated much travel detail. Besides, I don't like travel; it's such a hassle—buying tickets and finding hotels and arguing about where to change buses.

Tourists with backpacks and sandals are always saying, "You simply must see the Purple Phoenix Pagoda, it's incredible." So you get into a truck full of people and their sacks of grain and chickens, and after forty-five minutes you get off and walk through a lot of mud to find a concrete gazebo painted purple. Or a rock that an emperor in the Ming dynasty stood on when he made a speech. That's not my idea of enjoyment, so I didn't become a good collector of places when I was in China, and the places I did visit made very little impression on me.

On the other hand, I did remember all kinds of people who I thought were interesting. My memory is so bad that if something sticks there I figure it must be noteworthy. So, basically, all I did in my book was to write about the people I remembered. I didn't have a certain literary genre in mind or any idea of what I wanted to do with what I had written. When I sent off the last story to my editor I fully expected her to call and say, "O.K., this is a good start. Now it's time to make a book out of it," and I didn't know what I was going to do about that. Several people reminded me that every book should have a theme, a larger point. I couldn't think of any larger point about my stay in China except "There's no place like home."

Finally my editor came to see me. "All right, what

are we going to do with this?" she said. She spread all my little disconnected stories out on the floor. Then she said, "I've been thinking: What if we just string three or four of these episodes together and give them a chapter title? That will make people think you had it in mind as a chapter all along." So that's what we did. I can't honestly say, "Well, you see, I had in mind these small, jewel-like episodes that could be strung together."

If *Iron and Silk* qualifies as a travel book I'll have to expand my definition of travel writing to include books by people who go to unfamiliar places to live or to work, not just people who go as tourists. That way I can put my book in with pretty good company — some of my favorites fall within that definition, although you probably won't find them in the Travel section. *The Forest People*, by Colin Turnbull, is labeled Sociology and Anthropology; Turnbull spent three years in the Congo living with the Ba-Mbuti Pygmies and wrote a wonderful book about them. Another example would be Peter Freuchen's *Book of the Eskimos*, which I found under Ethnic Studies. Or how about Isak Dinesen's *Out of Africa*? That's usually found under Literature, along with William Least Heat Moon's *Blue Highways* and Beryl Markham's *West with the Night*. All these books could be called travel writing, but I think they are more about people than they are about places.

I'm an impatient reader as well as an impatient writer. I get bored by lengthy descriptions, which explains why I never liked nineteenth-century novels. *Tess of the D'Urbervilles* has about ninety pages of good story in it; all the rest is heath and flowers and strands of hair brushing against cheeks, and it puts me right to sleep. For me, a sense of place is nothing more than a sense of people. Whether a landscape is bleak or beautiful, it doesn't mean anything to me until a person walks into it, and then what interests me is how the person behaves in that place. To show you what I mean, I'd like to tell you a few "travel" stories.

My father is an amateur astronomer; stick him in a field on a clear night where there aren't any city lights nearby and he's a happy man. He used to wake us kids up in the middle of the night just to see some fuzzy speck through his telescope that he insisted was a globular cluster or a spiral galaxy. You can imagine how excited he was when he heard that in 1970 there was to be a total eclipse of the sun that would be visible along the coast of Virginia. For a year in advance he planned a drive down there from our home in Connecticut. He would spread maps all over the living room and just stare at them over and over, even though I-95 would take us the whole way.

Finally the big moment arrived. I was only ten and my brother was eight, but my father didn't want us to miss it. He woke us at one o'clock in the morning and put us in the back of the Volkswagen bus and we drove all night. It was such an adventure! I remember stopping at a gas station at around four in the morning so that Dad could fill his thermos with coffee. When you're a kid, just smelling coffee makes you feel grown-up. Smelling it in the middle of the night in a car on the highway made me feel like the ancient mariner.

We drove and drove, saw the sun come up in Maryland, and arrived at the Cape Charles beach at around ten-thirty. We had a few hours to kill, so my brother and I paced up and down the beach, collecting crab claws for our baby sister and poking at a gull skeleton that convinced us we were at the edge of the world. We waited and waited, and I wasn't exactly sure what we were waiting for because I was just a kid. I knew that something was going to happen to the sun, but I didn't know what. Well, we were just standing there, and all of a sudden we saw it coming across the ocean — the shadow. When the moon blocks out the sun it casts a shadow on the earth, and it was just our luck that the shadow was moving west, across the water and toward us. The shadow raced over the ocean like a wall of darkness. It was such a distinct line. The sky was full of gulls, and when that line of blackness hit them they dropped like stones into the water as if they had been shot, and went silent. It was the most extraordinary thing. The wall kept coming toward us, and then *boom!*

I don't know how many of you have seen a total eclipse, but what happens is that the whole sky goes ultramarine. It's like those paint sets you get as a kid. There's always a blue, and you use it to paint the sky, but it never looks like the sky — what sky is that blue? Well, *this* sky is that blue. It's so rich and deep that the stars come out, while the horizon is a luminous red. Overhead there's a soft white glow, and right in the middle of that is the blackest disk you've ever seen, which is the moon in front of the sun. It's pure science fiction.

Anyway, here it was, the moment of a lifetime, and I suddenly noticed that my father was talking to somebody. After all that planning and staring at all those Rand McNally maps he wasn't looking at the eclipse; he was pleading with a family that was standing right next to us. At the instant of totality these people had turned around and were facing the other way. Somebody had told them that if you look at an eclipse it will hurt your eyes, which isn't true; it's *before* totality that you mustn't stare at it. But when it's total all the harmful rays are blocked, and you're just missing the greatest thing in your life. So my father was pleading with these people: "Turn around! Look at it! It's safe, I promise you—I wouldn't let my children look at it if it wasn't safe!" And they thought he was some kind of nut. "Don't listen to that crazy man," the parents told their kids, and they waddled them away, off the beach. They never did turn around.

Of course the eclipse was spectacular, but if that had been the only thing that happened that day I don't think I would remember it so clearly. But the fact that this family came all the way to "see the eclipse" and then didn't dare look at it: the wasted opportunity made that velvet-black disk even more rare and spectacular. It also told me so much about my father. Totality only lasts about two minutes, and he wasted a minute of it trying to get those people to see it.

Here's another story. One of my martial arts teachers in Hunan was a Buddhist. He was a very religious man, and he asked me if I would go to a holy mountain south of the city and climb to the top, where there was a beautiful temple, and burn incense there for him. I said I would. When I got to the base of the mountain I wasn't feeling well and I found that it was a long hike to the summit. By then it was raining, which only made things worse. I would have preferred to just go home, but I knew that if I was going to get up there at all I would have to do it then. So I trudged up the mountain through the rain and mud for three or four hours. It was a miserable climb, and by the time I got to the top I was feverish and had a bad headache.

I found a little hostel connected to the temple, and two Buddhist nuns came to my room. They were practiced in traditional Chinese medicine and insisted on healing me with acupuncture. They told me to turn over and started jabbing harpoons into me. Those needles look small in the pictures, but when they start sticking them into you they look a lot bigger. They stuck the needles into the backs of my knees and into my temples and between my eyes, and every once in a while they would dig around with them and ask, "Do you have sensation?" At the end of the treatment they asked how I felt, and I said much better, but I only said it to get them out of my room. Actually I felt worse. When they left I took three aspirins, and then I did feel better.

Later the nuns came to check on me, and one of them asked what I was doing on the mountain. I explained that I had come to burn incense for my teacher. They said, "Well then, surely you'd like to meet the abbot of the monastery. He's a very holy man." I told them that that would be a great honor. They said, "We can arrange an introduction for you tomorrow. But you'll have to get up early."

The next morning I got up early and the nuns came and led me into the scroll room of the monastery. It was a beautiful room, filled with crimson lacquer scroll cabinets that held the Buddhist sutras. An assistant came in and poured two cups of hot water, which is called "white tea." It's considered the purest form of refreshment. Then the abbot came in, looking very impressive in saffron robes and sandalwood prayer beads. He spoke a dialect that I didn't understand, so the assistant explained that he would act as translator. "The abbot is very busy," the assistant said. "He doesn't have much time this morning. He will ask you one question and you will answer, and then the interview will be over."

You can imagine, after studying Chinese philosophy for so many years, how excited I became. Chinese and Japanese Buddhists are well known for bringing their disciples to enlightenment with a single *koan*, or metaphysical question. I tried to empty my mind and waited for his question. After drinking his white tea in silence the abbot spoke. When he was finished, the assistant nodded and turned to me. Furrowing his brow, he said, "The abbot wishes to know what your people did to Richard Nixon. Mr. Nixon was a friend of China, you know."

After I wrote *Iron and Silk* the book didn't actually come out for a year and a half, and when that period of waiting was almost up I got very nervous. I was sure the book was going to be a disaster, not because I didn't like it but because I had never thought of myself as a real writer. Real writers stay up late smoking French cigarettes and reading Sartre, whereas I'm usually in bed by ten and my idea of an existential dilemma is whether to watch "The Simpsons" or rent a Bruce Lee movie for the twentieth time. So when a man named Stuart Stevens called and said he wanted to travel the Silk Route in China and write a book about it and wanted me to go along, it seemed like a perfect opportunity to be out of the country when my book was published.

A month later we were in the Dunhuang caves in Gansu province. Dunhuang was one of the key oases along the Silk Route, starting around the Fifth Century A.D.; it was the last stop on the way out of China proper and marked the beginning of Chinese Turkestan. Wealthy, devout travelers commissioned religious statues and wall paintings there, either to gain

Buddha's protection before starting west across the Takla Makan Desert — the name means "Go in but don't come out" — or to thank Buddha for having already delivered them across it on their eastward trip. As a result of this two-way traffic, a unique style of art was born in Dunhuang and the other oases scattered across Turkestan — a subtle fusion of Indian, Chinese, Persian and Greek art from the time of Alexander the Great — that became known as Serindian art. This style gradually made its way east and was assimilated into mainstream Chinese art.

As the Chinese lost control of the region to the "barbarian" tribes of the northwest and as maritime trade routes improved, traffic along the Silk Route slowed. The sophisticated irrigation systems of the oases fell into disrepair, and around the tenth century A.D. the region fell into Islamic hands. Places like Dunhuang became ghost towns and many of them disappeared under the shifting sands of the desert.

When we visited Dunhuang the caves were officially closed for the winter, but we managed to tag along with an informal Chinese tour. One member of the tour was a young Chinese man with long hair, a mustache and a scruffy beard. He wore a battered pair of Levi's and a down jacket and carried a sketch pad. He preferred to linger out of earshot of our uninspired guide, where he could stare at the art in peace, taking notes and making quick sketches as he stroked his beard and nodded to himself. To my eyes, the most startling evidence of foreign influence in the Dunhuang art can be seen in the wall paintings that tell the stories of Buddhist saints' lives. The characters and the deities in these illustrated legends have very Chinese faces, and the strong emphasis on outlines and modulation of line is typical of Chinese painting. On the other hand, the use of shading to give three-dimensional mass to the figures and the graceful depiction of their bodies and clothing give them a sensuous realism that seems more Indian than Chinese.

As beautiful as the paintings were, I soon tired of our guide's lectures about the burgeoning socialist sensibilities of Wei Dynasty artists, so I wandered through a small passageway into a huge grotto dominated by a three-story-high stone Buddha. As I was looking at it the young man with the beard walked up beside me and said in Chinese, "This Buddha changes its expression depending on what time of day you look at it." He showed me that the cave was illuminated by whatever sunlight managed to trickle in through the small windows and tunnels above us. The morning light, he said, was different from the evening light and caused different shadows and highlights to appear on the Buddha's face.

"I've been here for three days," he explained, "and I come in with every tour so that I can see the caves as often as possible. That guide, by the way, doesn't know a thing. I even found a cave that isn't locked up at night, and I've been sleeping there. At night you can hear wild dogs barking, and you really feel like there are ghosts wandering around the caves."

I asked him why he was so interested in the caves. He told me that he was an artist from Beijing. "After I graduated from the fine arts academy there I started painting like all my classmates, imitating modern Western artists. That's the fad now in China — to try to paint like the abstract Western painters. But after a while I began to think that was all nonsense. So I thought, if I want to combine Western art with Chinese painting I should study Western art in its earliest forms and decide for myself what I want to do with it. So about six months ago I took all the money I had and started traveling west along the Silk Route. I have enough money to last another six months; by then I'll be in Kashgar and I can start painting again there."

Just then our guide came into the cave; apparently she had been looking for us. "You again!" she barked, pointing at the young painter. "I told you not to fall behind. You have to stay with the group. It's a regulation! No wandering around in the caves!" She folded her arms smartly and waited for us to leave. The painter looked at me and shook his head with amusement. Then he surreptitiously flashed me the peace sign as he led the way out of the cave.

It seemed a shame that this was the best access he could get to early "Western" painting — it looked entirely Eastern to me — and even more of a shame that he could see it only under the supervision of that tour guide. But he managed to keep his patience and his humor. Though I don't remember much about the three-story-high Buddha, I can see, as if it happened yesterday, that young Chinese painter flashing me the peace sign, an outdated gesture for Americans but a very current and powerful symbol of rebellion for him and his generation.

Later on that same trip, Stuart and I were in the Takla Makan Desert on our way to Kashgar, which is near the Afghanistan border. We were taking a three-day bus ride across the desert, and on the second day the bus broke down. Typical me, I groaned and predicted that we would be stuck there until the next bus came, which wouldn't be for a week. Stuart said, "Are you kidding? I'm going to stop an army truck and we'll ride with them." I said, "No way they'll stop for us." But pretty soon Stuart saw an army truck coming down the road — it was the only road for hundreds of miles in any direction — and stopped it by throwing himself on the hood. The driver got out. He was a Uighur — they're Turkish-speaking Moslems who constitute the majority of people living in Chinese Turkestan; many of them have light-colored hair, blue eyes and aquiline noses.

Stuart grabbed the driver and said to me, "Tell him he's going to take us to Kashgar." I said to the driver, "My friend thinks you're going to take us to Kashgar," and the driver, to my surprise, said O.K. But he said there was room for only one passenger in the front of the truck and he wanted me to sit up there because I could speak Chinese. Stuart had to get in the back, which was open, and roll himself up in a giant piece of canvas to protect himself from the cold.

We got started and the driver said, "There's something you must understand: I don't stop my truck. We will drive all night until we reach Kashgar." Kashgar was hundreds of miles away, through a desert that didn't have any gas stations; I didn't see how that was going to work. The driver said, "I am Ali, King of Trucks! I never stop my truck!"

And sure enough, several hours later when the gas gauge said empty, he asked me if I knew how to drive. I said I did. He handed me the wheel, opened the driver's side door, crawled out onto the running board and flung himself into the back of the truck, where he had two fifty-gallon drums. He sucked some gas into a tube to create a siphon and then stuck the tube into the gas tank. Meanwhile I kept driving the truck over a dirt road at forty miles an hour in pitch darkness.

Later that night Ali got drowsy, so he just curled up in his army coat and fell asleep. So here I was, driving a huge army truck through a totally desolate place; it looked like the surface of the moon, with no sign of vegetation or animal life. Suddenly we came to a military checkpoint — there are a lot of them in this region because the Takla Makan Desert is where China does most of its nuclear testing. The guard was a Han Chinese. I yelled at Ali and shook him, but he was out. The guard shined a flashlight in at me and I rolled the window down. "Where are you from?" he demanded. "Urumqi," I said, which is the capital of Xinjiang province. "Where are you going?" he asked. "Kashgar," I said. He asked me what sort of person I was. I told him I was a Uighur. He grunted and waved me on.

I thought that was the end of the adventure. But about an hour later the truck started to make strange noises and I saw that the engine temperature gauge was as high as it could go. I shook Ali awake and asked him what to do. "My radiator has a leak," he said. "I have to put water in it." I asked him if he had any water. "No," he said, "but that's no problem." With the truck still going, he got out and climbed up on the hood. "Never stop the truck!" he called back to me.

After a few minutes he climbed back down onto the running board and said, "Drive off the road here and make a slow circle and come back to the road up ahead. I'll meet you there." He pointed to where he wanted me to rejoin the road. Then he grabbed a couple of metal containers and jumped off the truck and ran across the sand. I saw that he had found a frozen riverbed. He broke the ice and filled the containers with water while I drove a slow circle in the desert. When I got back to the road he jumped up on the truck (I didn't stop), opened the hood, poured the icy water from the containers into the engine, closed the hood and swung himself back into the passenger seat. "I am Ali, King of Trucks!" he said, then went back to sleep.

The best piece of travel literature I know isn't a book. It's a documentary film called *For All Mankind*. The man who directed it is a writer who went to Houston ten years ago on the tenth anniversary of the moon landing. He visited NASA's film library and saw some footage that the astronauts shot during their trips to the moon and he thought, "Why doesn't anyone do something with all this?" So he spent ten years looking at six million feet of film and editing it and organizing it so that you feel you're along with the astronauts on their journey. The film begins with them putting on their space suits and takes them to the moon and back.

When I went to the movie I expected to be impressed by the photography and the magnitude of the whole thing—imagine watching a bunch of guys get strapped to a tower of explosives and ride it to the surface of the moon. I wasn't disappointed—I saw the movie six times in a row. But for me the most incredible moment wasn't the sight of the rocket taking off, or the moon getting closer, or even the earth getting farther away. It was seeing the astronauts on the surface of the moon, skipping like little boys and singing, "I was walking on the moon one day." Here they were, two superbly trained test pilots, goofing around to the point of stumbling and falling down, even though the slightest puncture in their suits would have killed them. In another scene you see the astronauts tossing pens back and forth in their zero-gravity spacecraft while technicians down on earth keep imploring them over the radio to get back to work. The astronauts say they were having so much fun they could hardly concentrate on flying the capsule.

They got to participate in the greatest travel adventure of all time, and you'd think they would have felt like heroes up there. But instead they say they felt insignificant. They saw that life as we know it is a thin film of activity stretched over a spinning rock hanging in the middle of limitless space. They say that time itself lost all meaning. And you can see it in the way they behave; their sense of the immediate fleeting moment transforms the simplest tasks like picking up rocks into unforgettable gestures. That's what really got to me — their sense of how precious that time was. I could watch a hundred hours of pictures of outer space and it wouldn't do much for me. But the sight of those men in their big white suits hopping on the moon gave me a real sense of place — of what I might have felt if I had been there myself. That's good travel literature.

VIVIAN GORNICK

# An American Woman in Egypt

For years I thought of my book *In Search of Ali Mahmoud* as the road not taken. It came to represent a kind of writing that I felt I had abandoned in fear and haste, turning away apprehensively from that which was difficult to pursue. This year I reread it for the first time since it was written in 1973, and I see that I've been stumbling along in darkness and confusion, plunging repeatedly off the shoulder, even wandering about in the underbrush, but in fact keeping parallel with the course this early "travel" set me on. The trip to Egypt was the beginning of a writing apprenticeship that has taken years to articulate itself and even more years to complete.

I began my working life as a writer of what in the sixties and seventies was called personal journalism, a hybrid term meaning part personal essay, part social criticism. I didn't set out to do this kind of writing; it just seemed natural from the minute I sat down at the typewriter to use myself—that is, to use my own response to a circumstance or an event—as a means of interpretation, of making some larger sense of things. At the time, of course, that was a shared instinct: many other writers felt similarly compelled. The personal had become political, and the headlines metaphoric. We all felt implicated. We all felt that immediate experience signified. Wherever a writer looked, there was a narrative line to be drawn from the political tale being told on a march, at a party, in an encounter. Three who did it brilliantly during those years were Joan Didion, Tom Wolfe and Norman Mailer.

I went to work at the *Village Voice* in 1969. Inclined by nature toward polemics and now on the barricades for radical feminism, I welcomed the instinct to put on paper the sound of my own voice to tell the story and make the point. True, the point was political, but mine was a politics that grew directly out of original experience. That connection was a vital one, never to be lost. The analysis was always to emerge out of my "own hurt feelings"—an old political injunction. The *Voice* and I were made for each other.

From the beginning I saw the dangers of this kind

of writing — saw what skill and clarity it would take to maintain the right balance between me and the story, to not mistake myself for the subject, to keep my eye on the target. Personal journalism had already thrown up many examples of people rushing into print with no clear idea of the relation between narrator and subject. Writers often struck the wrong note: one of confessionalism, or therapy, or simple self-absorption.

I don't know how well or how consistently I practiced what I had begun to preach to myself, but I was always aware of the problem. I took it as my task to keep myself subordinated to the idea in hand. The point was never to devolve on me. I was never to tell an anecdote, fashion a description, indulge a speculation that had myself at the center. I was to use myself only to clarify the argument, develop the analysis, push the story forward. I thought my grasp of the situation accurate and my self-consciousness sufficient. The reliable reporter in me would guarantee the trustworthy narrator.

In 1971 a book editor approached me with an idea that struck a note of response. She invited me to go to the Middle East and write about "the Arabs," as she put it. I said no, not the Middle East; Egypt, only Egypt. I would go to Egypt and write about middle-class Cairenes. She agreed, and we struck a deal. A month later I was landing at the Cairo airport.

Why Egypt? A few years before, I had fallen in love with an Egyptian engineer, a Fulbright student at Berkeley. He had grown up on the streets of Cairo, I on the streets of New York. We found ourselves a pair of educated, street-smart urchins, alike in ways that surprised and gratified us both. He pined for Cairo, this soft, sad, tender-hearted stranger in America, and told me often how the letters from his mother brought him the city, and this sustained him. Those letters from his mother. He would read them to me, and I'd say, "More, read more." The woman in the letters was immensely appealing, wise and sympathetic. Once she wrote, "I fear for you, my son, when I think of you remaining in the United States. You *know* what they think of us," and I remember thinking, Who *are* these people? That's why Egypt.

I assumed that I would do in Cairo what I had been doing at the *Village Voice* for two years. I would put myself down in the middle of the city, meet all these Egyptians, turn them into "encounters," use my own fear and prejudice to let them become themselves, and then I'd make something of it, arrive at point.

But Cairo was not the *Village Voice*, and personal

journalism turned out to be not exactly the right job description.

I spent six months in Egypt, living in Cairo all that time, traveling wherever I was permitted and whenever possible. I was always working. Morning, noon and night I was with Egyptians: doctors, lawyers, housewives, journalists, students, guides, friends, neighbors, lovers. Everyone took me out, and everyone took me home. It was nonstop family life, nonstop street life, nonstop conversation. Nonstop. That's how I remember Egypt.

The engineer and I had been right about ourselves: we each came from one of the great cities of the world and we were both urban to the core. For me, Cairo was New York, a bombardment of stimuli — filthy, dusty, crowded, alive and in pain, constantly reactive, always in motion. And the people: dark, nervous, intelligent, ignorant and tender, volatile and needy. Familiar. Somehow, very familiar. The familiarity was my downfall. It excited and confused me. I fell in love with it, and I romanticized it. That is, I romanticized its seeming mysteriousness. Who was I? Who were they? Where *was* I, and what was it all about? The problem was, I didn't really want the answers to these questions. I thought the "unknowingness" of things was alluring. I thought it fine to lose myself in it. But when one makes a romance out of unknowingness it's hard to arrive at point. The reliable reporter was in danger of becoming the untrustworthy narrator. And to a large degree she did.

When I reread the book this year I was gratified to see how hardworking that reporter had actually been. I was reminded of how marvelous a people the Egyptians had been in my eyes, and how rich and vivid was the city of Cairo. They are both there on the page in all their crowded, noisy life — and I moving steadily among them, knowing each day that I had to get it down, get it down, worry later about what it all meant. And thank God I did. If it hadn't been for the extensiveness of my notes . . .

Those notes. I worked on long sheets of yellow lined paper and kept a file on each person I knew. After a while I taped these files to the walls of my study-bedroom, and as the months went on they extended farther down the walls. Once a Cairo journalist followed me into the room as I rushed ahead looking for something on my desk. He stopped talking in mid-sentence. I turned around. He was staring at the long strips of paper. I saw in his eyes that he was thinking, She works for the CIA. Then he said softly, "For informations you would sell your grandmother, yes?" A few months ago this same man was in New York. I hadn't seen him in eighteen years. When he called he asked if I was married. I told him no so dryly he cried out, "Oh, Vivi-yaan, you were such a beautiful girl, do not tell me you are one of these American feminists hates men!"

No, Aziz, I won't tell you I'm one of these American feminists hates men.

I heard his voice and Egypt came back in a rush. This Aziz and I used to walk the streets of Cairo together for hours, stopping only now and then for coffee. In the worst heat Aziz, then a slim young man with a headful of black curls, wore a tight pin-striped suit. He'd mop his forehead and tell me feverishly about the awfulness of his life: the pain, the hunger, the spiritual deprivation. I was always struck by how intelligent he was — and how he never came to any conclusion about anything he said. I'd nod as we walked, asking all the right questions so that he would keep talking, and finally I'd say, "So? What do you make of it?" He'd look at me, shrug his shoulder eloquently and say, "What I should make of it? Don't you understand? This is the *life!* Our life!"

There was another Egyptian who also often said to me, "Don't you understand, this is the life, our life." She was a tall, elegant woman who ran a business and a household with skill and dispatch. One day when I was visiting her, her brother, his wife and their children came to call. The whole family seemed listless and depressed. After a prolonged cup of coffee they left. My friend sighed and said, "It is a difficult time for them. He wished to leave her, but this we cannot permit." I asked what she meant and she said, "He has fallen in love with the wife of my uncle, and we are all opposed to it. We called a family council and we gave him our decision. He cried out against us at first, but now we are in negotiations, as you say. That is why he comes to see me now, once a week, as a family."

I was surprised, and I asked many questions. A picture emerged of family interference at a high level. I asked my friend how she had discovered the affair between her brother and the wife of her uncle, as she put it. She told me that the previous spring there had been a family gathering at a farm they all owned not far from Cairo. At the gathering she had made orange juice. The oranges were not sweet enough, so she added sugar. "When my uncle came," she said, "his wife drank some juice and said, 'This has sugar in it.' Yes, I replied, and thought no more of it. Then my brother came. He took a glass of juice, and as he was about to drink she laid her hand on his arm and said, 'Do not drink this. It has sugar in it.' He put the glass down. I thought, Why does he do as she tells him to do? What is between these two? After that it was just a matter of watching and waiting."

I listened, astonished as always by the Egyptian capacity to observe human behavior. From the littlest child to the oldest grandfather one saw continually what amounted to a novelist's ability to observe shrewdly and describe wonderfully. After a while I asked my friend what she made of such extraordinary primacy of family involvement. What did she think it meant, this lifelong embroilment of brothers and sisters, mothers and fathers? Where did it lead, what were its consequences? She, like Aziz, said to me, "What should I make of it? This is the life! Our life!" But she said it with an intensity that burned a hole in the conversation. She reminded me of the beginning of my stay in Egypt. I was always being reminded of the beginning.

On my first day in Cairo I wandered into a café across the street from the main municipal building and looked around. I was the only woman in the room. The men — mostly lawyers and government clerks — were all wearing tight black or brown pin-striped suits and horn-rimmed glasses, carrying briefcases, smoking passionately, talking loudly and with that amazing intensity. I thought, Where have I seen this before? Then I realized that it reminded me of Dostoevsky's St. Petersburg. This is what it must have been like on the eve of the revolution, this pressure-cooker intensity everywhere.

Intelligent fever. The whole country was in an intelligent fever. I loved them for it. They touched me to the heart. I thought their condition profound, and I identified with it. Instead of analyzing my subject I merged with my subject. The Egyptians and I became one. They were nervous, I was nervous. They were needy, I was needy. They were neurotic, I was neurotic.

It's interesting to me to see exactly how I picked up on this essential aspect of Egyptian life. Every Egyptian man saw himself as a tragic hero, condemned to live out his life being dismissed and despised, powerless and rejected. They were drowning in anxiety, and they loved themselves for it. They thought it made them poetic. I got right into it. I, too, loved my anxiety, dramatized it as much as they did, saw my neediness as proof of sensitivity.

Such identification in writing has its uses and its difficulties, and in my book on Egypt the narration reflects both. On the one hand, the prose is an amazement of energy, crowded with description and responses. On the other hand, the sentences are often rhetorical in construction, the tone ejaculatory, the syntax overloaded. Where one adjective will do, three are sure to appear. Where quiet would be useful, agitation fills the page. The book does this curious thing: it mimics Egypt itself. That is its strength and its limitation.

The problem was detachment: I didn't have any. I didn't even know it was something to be prized — that, in fact, it was crucial, that without detachment there can be no story. Description and response yes, but no story. When I had been a working journalist at the *Village Voice*, polemics had provided me with ready-made detachment. But now, in Egypt, I was somewhere else, out on my own, confused by a kind of writing whose requirements I didn't understand but whose power I felt jerked around by. It would be years — fifteen, in fact — before I sat down to write feeling that I had enough detachment to control the material — to describe and respond, and also arrive at point.

*Fierce Attachments*, the book that emerged, is a story about my mother, myself and a woman who lived next door to us when I was growing up. Actually that's the situation, not the story. The story is about the impossibility of leaving childhood. This is how it begins:

I'm eight years old. My mother and I come out of our apartment onto the second floor landing. Mrs. Drucker is standing in the open doorway of the apartment next door, smoking a cigarette. My mother locks the door and says to her, "What are you doing here?" Mrs. Drucker jerks her head backward toward her own apartment. "He wants to lay me. I told him he's gotta take a shower before he can touch me." I know that "he" is her husband. "He" is always the husband. "Why? He's so dirty?" my mother says. "He feels dirty to *me*," Mrs. Drucker says. "Drucker, you're a whore," my mother says. Mrs. Drucker shrugs her shoulder. "I can't ride the subway," she says. In the Bronx "ride the subway" was a euphemism for going to work.

I lived in that tenement between the ages of six and twenty-one. There were twenty apartments, four to a floor, and all I remember is a building full of women. I hardly remember the men at all. They were everywhere, of course — husbands, fathers, brothers — but I remember only the women. And I remember them all crude like Mrs. Drucker or fierce like my mother. They never spoke as though they knew who they were, understood the bargain they had struck with life, but they often acted as though they knew. Shrewd, volatile, unlettered, they performed on a Dreiserian scale. There would be years of apparent calm, then suddenly an outbreak of panic and wildness: two or three lives scarred (perhaps ruined), and the turmoil would subside. Once again: sullen quiet, erotic torpor, the ordinariness of daily denial. And I — the girl growing in their midst, being made in their image — I absorbed them as I would chloroform on a cloth laid against my face. It has taken me thirty years to understand how much of them I understood.

That voice told the story I wanted to tell. That voice *was* the story I wanted to tell. For two years I sat at the typewriter, listening for the sound of that voice. When it filled my head, I wrote. When I lost it, I sat immobilized. The situation was a good one, but the story was everything. The woman who went to Egypt had a situation; the woman who wrote *Fierce Attachments* had a story. The question is: Could she have gotten to the story without the trip to Egypt?

In every work of literature there's both a situation and a story. The situation is the context or circumstance, sometimes the plot; the story is the emotional experience that preoccupies the writer. In *An American Tragedy* the situation is Dreiser's America; the story is the nature of desire. In Edmund Gosse's memoir *Father and Son* the situation is fundamentalist England in the time of Darwin; the story is the power of unexpected tenderness. In a poem called "In the Waiting Room" Elizabeth Bishop describes herself at the age of seven, during the First World War, sitting in a dentist's office, turning the pages of *National Geographic*, listening to the muted cries of pain her timid aunt utters from within. That's the situation. The story is a child's first experience of isolation: her own, her aunt's, and that of the world.

Actually the memoirist has more in common with the poet than with the novelist. The novelist says, "I see the world, and through my characters I will make sense of it." The poet says, "I see the world, and through my own naked response I will make sense of it." Augustine's *Confessions* remains a model for the memoirist. He tells the story of his conversion to Christianity. That's the situation. In this tale he moves from an inchoate sense of being to a coherent sense of being, from an idling existence into a purposeful one, from a state of ignorance to a state of truth. That's the story. Inevitably it's a story of self-discovery and self-definition.

The subject of autobiography is always self-definition, but it can't be self-definition in the void. The memoirist, like the poet and the novelist, must engage with the world, because engagement makes experience, experience makes wisdom, and finally it's the wisdom that counts. "Good writing has two characteristics," a gifted teacher of writing once said. "It's alive on the page, and the reader is persuaded that the writer is on a voyage of discovery." The poet, the novelist, the memoirist all must convince the reader that they have wisdom and are writing as honestly as possible to arrive at what they know. Unavoidably the reader asks, "Is this voice speaking truth? Is it honestly going somewhere?" In other words, is the narrator trustworthy?

How does a narrator become trustworthy?

While I was writing *Fierce Attachments* I read a monograph by Raymond Williams on George Orwell. Williams was mainly interested in analyzing Orwell's politics, but in the middle of the piece he wrote two brilliant paragraphs on how George Orwell created "George Orwell." What Williams said, in essence, was that in a writer like Orwell, point of view is everything. It amounts to persona. It's the equivalent of narrative drive. It determines shape and direction to a crucial extent, becomes in fact the world of the writing. We only need to recall the first page and a half of Orwell's *Shooting an Elephant* to know what Williams is talking about. There, interspersed among paragraphs of introductory description, Orwell writes:

In Moulmein, in Lower Burma, I was hated by large numbers of people — the only time in my life I have been important enough for this to happen to me. . . . In the end the sneering yellow faces that met me everywhere, the insults hooted after me when I was at a safe distance, got badly on my nerves. The young Buddhist priests were the worst. . . . All I knew was that I was stuck between my hatred of the empire I served and my rage against the evil-spirited little beasts who tried to make my job impossible. With one part of my mind I thought of the British Raj as something clamped down upon the will of prostrate peoples; with another part I thought that the greatest joy in the world would be to drive a bayonet into a Buddhist priest's guts.

The man who speaks those sentences *is* the story being told. The fusion of experience, perspective and personality contained in that voice becomes an instrument of illumination. Because we know who is speaking, we understand what is being said. All that intelligent murderousness brought to the point of *helpless* truth-speaking is what *Shooting an Elephant* is all about. The writer experiences something outside himself, but the way in which he experiences it becomes the subject as much as the thing being examined. This, in nonfiction as well as in fiction, is world revealed through self. The presence of the writer makes the essay literature.

From journalism to the essay to the memoir: the trip being taken by a nonfiction writer deepens and turns ever more inward.

One of the most interesting memoirists of our time is another Englishman, J. R. Ackerley. When Ackerley died in 1967, at seventy-one, he left behind a remarkable piece of confessional writing he had been working on for the better part of thirty years, called *My Father and Myself*. Ostensibly it's a tale of family life. Ackerley grew up the son of Roger Ackerley, a fruit merchant known most of his life as "the banana king." This father was a large, easygoing, generous man, at once expansive and reticent, kindly but indirect in his manner, most indirect. Ackerley himself grew up to become literary and homosexual, absorbed with his own interests and secrets, given to hiding his real life from the family. After his father's death in 1929 Ackerley learned that Roger had lived a double life. All the time the Ackerleys were growing up in middle-class comfort in Richmond, the father was keeping a second family on the other side of London: a mistress and three daughters. The disclosure of this "secret orchard," as the Victorian euphemism had it, astounded Joe Ackerley to such a degree that he became obsessed with probing deeper into the obscurity of his father's beginnings. In time he became convinced that in his youth Roger had also been a male whore, and that it was through the love of a wealthy man that he had gained his original stake in life.

This is the story J. R. Ackerley set out to tell. Why did it take him thirty years to tell it? Why not three? Because what I've told you was not his story, it was his situation. His story was what took thirty years to get to.

*My Father and Myself* is little more than two hundred pages long. Its prose is simple, lucid, direct. It's wonderfully inviting from the first, now-famous sentence: "I was born in 1896 and my parents were married in 1919." That voice will address with grace and candor whatever it is necessary to examine. From it will flow strong feeling and vivid intelligence. The distance it achieves is just right: not too close, not too far. At this distance everyone and everything is interesting, or at least understandable.

Ackerley was, he thought, putting together a puzzle of family life. All I have to do, he said to himself, is get the sequence right and the details correct and everything will fall into place. But nothing fell into place. After a while he thought, I'm not describing a presence, I'm describing an absence. This is the story of an unlived relationship. Who was he? Who was I? Why did we keep missing each other? After another while he realized, I always thought my father didn't want to know me. Now I see I didn't want to know *him*. And then he realized, It's not him I haven't wanted to know, it's myself.

It took Ackerley thirty years to clarify the voice that could tell this story — thirty years to gain detachment, thirty years to make an honest man of himself, become a trustworthy narrator — and you can trace that clarifying process paragraph by paragraph, sentence by sentence, incident by incident. Ackerley as I have experienced him in writings *about* him often seems nasty or pathetic. But the Ackerley speaking in *My Father and Myself* is a wholly engaging man — not because he sets out to be fashionably honest but because the reader feels him struggling with something important. The writer in him kept working to free the voice that would keep stripping down anxiety to get at the thing underneath. Ackerley may not have the powers of a poet, but in *My Father and Myself* he certainly has the intent.

My trip to Egypt and the book that emerged from it now seem to me an embodiment of my own struggle to clarify, to release from anxiety, the narrator who could serve the situation and tell the story. In Egypt it was my instinct to make my voice an "instrument of illumination." The decision to put myself down as a character among characters was this instinct in disguise, but I wasn't able to do so — not, I think, because of lack of skill, although it may also have been that (I really believe skill serves readiness), but because it was a time when my own psychological wishes were so mixed as to make it impossible that instinct be obeyed. I wanted both to clarify and to mystify. My intent was compromised: it never became simply available to me.

What is interesting to me now when I read the book is to see this writer's dilemma being laid out on the page, and at the same time to see how Egypt and the Egyptians keep taking it away from me. They overrun the situation. The country and the people were so strong, so vivid, so immensely alive within themselves that they fought successfully for the lion's share of the space. And I never grudged them a line of it. This is a book in which subject, reporter and narrator are unevenly matched but ultimately well suited. Someday I'd like to go back to Egypt and take another look at it — and at myself *in* it. That would be another story. One thing's for sure: it wouldn't be just a situation.

CALVIN TRILLIN

# Traveling in America

In the late sixties, when a lot of people were talking about a sense of community, I realized that my community consisted of traveling people — regional auditors, traveling salesmen, people crossing the state line to advocate the overthrow of the government by force and violence. I had begun what was to become fifteen years of traveling around the United States, writing a piece every three weeks for *The New Yorker* under the heading "U.S. Journal." Jules Loh of the Associated Press had a similar assignment — he did a shorter column that appeared more frequently — and we formed an organization called the American Association of American Reporters Covering America. Our acronym was GLINGPAC. We just kind of liked the way GLINGPAC sounded.

Jules and I were the only members. Our organization had only one rule: you can't quote de Tocqueville. That's how we kept the membership down. The headquarters of the American Association of American Reporters Covering America — or what we preferred to think of as HQ GLINGPAC — was, of course, O'Hare Airport.

What I was trying to do in "U.S. Journal," I eventually decided, was to write about the country without concentrating on the government and politics of the country. Although the series I was doing used place names in its headlines — say, "U.S. Journal: El Paso, Texas" — it was not meant to be directly about places. I went to specific stories; the one in El Paso had to do with a bitter strike in a pants factory. But as a rule the story was told in the context of the place. And the piece only worked if the reader learned something about the place in addition to finding out what had happened there.

During those fifteen years, for instance, I did two stories on librarians being fired. The controversies were actually fairly similar, but the stories were not at all alike. One of them took place in East Hampton, Long Island. The cast of characters in that one included a group of people known as "the Maidstone crowd," after the Maidstone Club, which I described as a club that has managed to maintain its social purity so well that the name "Maidstone" is identified primarily with the worldly accomplishments of East Hampton residents who wouldn't be permitted to belong. Also involved was a group known by the splendid and revealing name of "year-round summer people" and a group known to the Maidstone crowd as "old East Hampton families" — people who in another community might have been called the Main Street business crowd.

The second library story took place in Fairhope, Alabama, which was founded in the nineteenth century as a Utopian community by the followers of Henry George, a reformer who believed in a single tax on land. Fairhope still has residents whose families settled there as Single Taxers or as one variety or another of the mavericks and freethinkers tolerated by the early Single Taxers, but it has even more people who live there because it's convenient to Mobile or because it has a reputation as a safe and pleasant place to retire. Fairhope, like East Hampton, is on the shore, but it's not a place familiar with creatures called year-round summer people. East Hampton is smaller than Fairhope, but it's not the sort of place where members of the library board might, as Fairhope library board members had, resent a librarian partly because they felt that she was treating them like yokels.

When I started on my travels, in 1967, the conventional wisdom was that the United States was becoming homogenized. It was said that the same franchise-heavy double-lane highways were everywhere, that everybody knew the same television sitcom jokes and that the regions of America had been fused into one. To a great extent that was true — there was a lot of similarity in American cities in the sixties, particularly in the area I sometimes thought of as the Expansion Team United States — the part of the country that didn't have major league baseball before the Second World War. In that part of the country, civic leaders all seemed eager to live in a big-league city and they had what amounted to a checklist of what was required for major league status. It included an international airport and a symphony orchestra and a domed stadium and any number of restaurants circling around on top of bank buildings and, naturally, a major league franchise.

In those days the civic boosters I met in various American cities had an attitude toward New York that reminded me of those passages in Russian novels in which people always ask, "What's happening in the capital?" A lot of people in American cities — particularly the people who had some control over other people's bond money — judged themselves and their town by the standards of New York, although they were quick to say that as a place to live they would prefer Yakutsk, Siberia, over Manhattan.

At some point in the seventies, however, people began to accept the authenticity of their home territory. They started bragging about their regional theater instead of about the number of touring Broadway musicals that had come through. They started restoring old buildings that had something to do with the history of the place instead of trying to put up the fourth highest building west of the Mississippi without windows. They started taking pride in the regional food they had always enjoyed instead of leading all visitors to the restaurant I had begun to refer to as La Maison de la Casa House, Continental Cuisine.

But even these efforts could make places look pretty much alike. The sameness of design clichés in the districts thought of as "olde" were only slightly less relentless than the ubiquitous golden arches on the double-lane highways — a theme I dealt with in a piece called "Thoughts After Prolonged Exposure to Exposed Brick." Writing about one restored shopping center, Quincy Market on the Boston waterfront, I said that "a vegetable stand is likely to be identified by a hand-carved slab of wood, or by a piece of black-and-white graphic art that to my untutored eye appeared to be a sixteenth-century radish."

The hotels that we traveling people stayed in also seemed to change more or less in lockstep. At one point there was a sudden infusion of what we thought of as boffo-lobby hotels. That trend was started by John Portman, in Atlanta, in the Hyatt Regency, which had a twenty-one-floor atrium lobby and a glass elevator that, as they said in Atlanta, went clean through the roof. The boffo-lobby hotels at least provided entertainment for traveling people — an opportunity to skip the Esther Williams movie on television and spend the evening flicking peanuts off the balconies onto the people walking around below. The Hyatt Regency quickly became the symbol of Atlanta, which meant that, like such civic symbols as the Golden Gate Bridge and the Empire State Building, it drew the showier suicides. People who worked in the lobby told me they felt as if they were in the blitz.

Then we got a flurry of hotels that I thought of as the "little touches" hotels. They were usually in older downtown buildings that had been gutted and done over in a lot of polished wood and shiny brass — a style that I called overstated understatement. They specialized in little touches — newspapers outside your door in the morning, designer soap, terry-cloth robes, terry-cloth robes with hoods (a little touch on a little touch), free shoeshines if you left your shoes outside your door before going to bed. I was reluctant to leave my shoes outside the door. I once heard that on a state visit to Washington the president of Finland left his shoes outside his door — he was staying in Blair House, across from the White House — and woke up the next morning to find that they had been donated to the Salvation Army.

Superficially, then, places in America, particularly cities, had a certain sameness during the years I was on the road. In fact, there were times when I didn't know which city I was in. Sometimes I would leave home on Sunday night to fly to wherever I intended to spend my week. I'd rent a car at the airport, drive to my destination, get a room at a motel and turn in. The next morning I'd wake up and look out the window at a strip of fast-food restaurants and realize that for a moment I didn't know where I was. I also had no idea which car was mine. I had to wait for all the traveling salesmen to leave before I could start my day.

When I was in college I took a course called Daily Themes, which required a short piece of fiction, a one-page vignette, every day. Actually it was every weekday; we had weekends off. Course grades were expressed in numbers, but until Daily Themes instructors were required to produce a numerical grade for the registrar, they used a marking system of their own: A, B, C, D and W. Nobody knew for certain what W meant, but most people thought it stood for Worthless. The instructors were generous with W's. The main part of the course consisted of conferences at which an instructor would explain to you, in some detail, why the themes you had turned in that week were so awful. But university rules also required a lecture, and the lecturers had a few slogans that they would chalk on the blackboard. One of them was "Individualize by Specific Detail," which I think is a useful slogan for anybody writing anything. Recently I looked through some of the "U.S. Journal" pieces for examples of using specific details. Here, for instance, is the way I described two different bars. The first passage is about a bar in Monticello, Iowa. I used it in a piece about how the most disreputable person in Center Junction, Iowa, came to shoot the most disreputable person in Maquoketa, Iowa:

Lou's Place, identified by a Hamm's Beer sign on a side street in Monticello, has a beer-company decor. There is a Schlitz clock, a Miller's clock, and three Hamm's clocks. Calendars are by Budweiser, Pabst, and Hamm's; lamps by Pabst, Hamm's, and Schlitz. About the only objects of non-brewery art are three tapestries — peacocks, mountain goats, and horses — that Lou (Louise Garrett) bought once from a foreign-looking traveling man. In Lou's Place, people often argue in loud voices and men use bad language in front of women, who use bad language back. But the most abusive customer can usually be put out by a barmaid, who may be only five feet two but has the advantage of being sober, of having put out a number of similarly abusive customers in the past, and of holding the power to refuse service indefinitely.

The second bar, which was in Miami, figured in a piece I wrote about a criminal lawyer named Harvey St. Jean, who also was murdered. St. Jean had built a reputation as a criminal lawyer and had then turned to divorce law; as he moved up the ladder he did his best to live the good life of South Florida:

A divorce lawyer who lived at the Jockey Club could feel as secure about his future as a dentist who lived in Hershey, Pennsylvania. The standing joke at the Jockey Club is that the average age of the residents is forty — "that's a sixty-year-old guy and a twenty-year-old broad." The club consists of a couple of high rises full of condominiums for the live-in members, some tennis courts, a marina in which some of the boats seem large enough to serve as destroyer escorts, a restaurant, and a bar whose patrons are so uniformly the type of people who order drinks by brand ("J & B and a twist, Joe, and an extra-dry Tanqueray martini") that the bartender's reaction to being asked for a Scotch-and-soda is likely to be a moment of puzzlement, as if he had just been asked for a jug of homemade busthead.

Looking through some of the "U.S. Journal" pieces, though, I find that I rarely tried to give a sense of place through passages that are thick with detail. More often I tried to begin — sometimes in the first sentence — by giving some hint what a place was like in a single sentence. This is the first sentence of a piece I did in Fairfield, Iowa, about a refugee family of Hmong tribesmen who tried to commit suicide together: "As a refuge, Fairfield, Iowa, has a lot going for it." This is about Bayou La Batre, on the Gulf Coast of Alabama, where my story was about the purchase of some industrial land by the Unification Church: "Bayou La Batre is thought of as a place where a lot of people are related to a lot of other people, none of whom bother to move inland as a hurricane approaches." This is about a neighborhood where a little girl died of child abuse: "They met in Cleveland, Tennessee, on the southeast side of town, a neighborhood that attracts some rural people who wander into Cleveland from the hill counties to work in furniture factories and some local people like Ronnie Maddox who never seem to work very long anywhere."

This is about Biddeford, Maine, where the people

who had political control of the town, descendants of French-Canadian mill workers, used the power of eminent domain to take the rich summer people's beach away from them: "Biddeford is virtually a French city, but nobody has ever thought of calling it the Paris of New England." This is about Nampa, Idaho: "A fertile agricultural area not far from Boise, Canyon County now has a number of food-processing plants which keep the economy fairly healthy and, on certain evenings, make the clear western air of Nampa smell like 85 million potato peels." This is about Grundy County, Iowa: "The soil in Grundy County is often spoken of as the richest soil in Iowa — which means, Grundy County residents sometimes add, that it must be about the richest soil in the world." And this is about San Antonio: "San Antonio is just about the only city in Texas that anybody has ever accused of being charming."

My intention in these sentences was not to attempt to sum up an entire place in a single phrase. I simply wanted to nudge readers in the right direction. I wanted to furnish them with a little foundation that they could use to build what I hoped would be a sort of structure. As the article progressed, of course, I provided more and more material for that structure. Before the Hmong family arrived in Fairfield, Iowa, for instance, the town had accommodated, without any great stress, an enterprise called Maharishi International University, where students were said to be instructed in arts that included human levitation. Bayou La Batre was, on the other hand, a place where residents, it was said, "don't even like strangers, let alone Moonies."

One of the reasons I didn't depend more on detailed physical description, I think, is that what was distinctive about a place for my purposes sometimes didn't show. When I first did a piece that was set in the part of Los Angeles called Watts—this was before the riots, so the name carried no connotations—I found that Los Angeles was one of those rare cities where a slum may be easier to identify by statistics than by walking through it. Sometimes a strong part of the character of a place is historical. In writing about New Orleans, I discussed the old question of whether New Orleans could be described as an American city:

New Orleans has traditionally nurtured some distinctly non-American attributes, like indolence. There have always been a good number of people who are not eager to get ahead. Even its businessmen have had a reputation for being only mildly industrious and distinctly non-entrepreneurial. New Orleans has been known as a place content to make do with its natural endowments—a great port on the Mississippi River, and a share of the state oil money, and a reputation for wickedness and charm that drew a steady stream of tourists for decades. For most of this century, New Orleans hasn't done much more than make do. It has never made a fetish out of equipping schools or paving streets. It has always had a lot of poor people; its rich people have never been seriously rich.

Later in that piece, I wrote, "Early on, New Orleans established an atmosphere of laissez-faire, and sometimes I think that by now there aren't enough Southern Baptists in the world to reverse that." There I was leaning on a theory propounded some years ago by Wilbur Zelinsky, a distinguished regionalist at Pennsylvania State University — the "doctrine of first effective settlement." It holds that the first people who establish themselves in a place set a tone that isn't likely to be altered, even when people from different backgrounds move in. Thus the attitude toward, say, liquor or the Republican Party in certain counties of Missouri may have a lot to do with whether the first settlers were from western New York or eastern Tennessee. My favorite use of Zelinsky's doctrine — stated by someone who presumably had never heard of the doctrine or of Zelinsky — is the theory of the dumbest sons. According to this theory, there was a time when a number of wealthy eastern families assigned their dumbest sons — the one who was of no use in the bank or the factory — to a life of coupon clipping in Santa Fe, New Mexico, and everything that has happened since in the ruling circles of Santa Fe can be traced to either the customs or the genes brought from the East by those founding offspring.

When I tried to describe a place I often tried to describe it according to what people do there, or how they feel about it, or how they feel about themselves. One of the advantages a reporter from outside has is that he can often hear a word or a phrase or a way of talking that local people have listened to so often that they no longer notice it. In Rockford, Illinois, for instance, it struck me that people often talked about negativism, in the way college students in the fifties used to discuss apathy — as an endemic, mildly regrettable, permanent condition. "A visitor to Rockford," I wrote, "is often reminded that Rockford is the second-largest city in Illinois, but the tone of voice used for the reminder is not exactly boastful, or even ironic (a city of 150,000 is, after all, a poor second to Chicago) but — well, negative: a tone that implies some disappointment that Rockford is all that the second-largest city in Illinois amounts to."

At other times I tried to give the sense of a place by talking about where it was. There is a special remoteness, for instance, that exists in a section of the southeastern California desert which is so sparsely populated that signs at the city limits don't say something like "City of Churches" but "Next Town 65 Miles." There can be a different sense of remoteness in a rural county that is far from the power centers of the state. I once did a piece in Clark County, Missouri, which is jammed into the northeast corner of Missouri, a couple of hundred miles from the state capital, the state university, the agricultural extension service and the site of the state fair. The nearest big town is in Iowa and so is the nearest important football team. The nearest daily newspapers are in Iowa and Illinois. People in Clark County can easily acquire the feeling that the rest of the people in Missouri aren't acutely aware of them.

Obviously, whatever device I used, I was working toward the same end. I was trying to give some idea of what was different about the place, what distinguished it from all other places, what was special about it. Often I used a number of different devices. In 1969 I did a piece in eastern Kentucky about the murder of a documentary filmmaker by an eccentric old man who was enraged to find filmmakers on his land. The piece has a long, detailed passage describing the courthouse of Harlan County, Kentucky, where the trial took place. It also has some discussion of the history of the area — the history of exploitation in the coal counties of eastern Kentucky, the history of violence that gave Harlan County the name of Bloody Harlan. Finally, it tried to give a sense of the place by simply recording a conversation between two women who were sitting in the courtroom, right after the old man's trial. One was the clerk of the court, a strong-looking woman with a strong Kentucky accent. The other was a woman who had come to know the filmmakers, a woman with a softer accent and a less certain tone to her voice:

"You know, I asked those men yesterday morning if they were happy with the outcome," the clerk said. "And they said, 'Yes.' And I said, 'Well, you know, us hillbillies is a queer breed. We are. I'm not offering any apologies when I say that. Us hillbillies *are* a queer breed, and I'm just as proud as punch to be one.'"

"Not all of us are like that," the other woman said. "Mean like that."

"Well, I wouldn't say that man is mean," the clerk said. "I don't guess he ever harmed anybody in his life. They were very nice people. I think it was strictly a case of misunderstanding. I think that the old man thought they were laughing and making fun of him, and it was more than he could take. I know this: a person isolated in these hills, they often grow old and eccentric, which I think they have a right to do."

"But he didn't have a right to kill," the other woman said.

"Well, no," the clerk said. "But us hillbillies, we don't bother nobody. We go out of our way to help people. But we don't want nobody pushin' us around. Now, that's the code of the hills. And he felt like—that old man felt like—he was being pushed around. You know, it's like I told those men: 'I wouldn't have gone on that old man's land to pick me a mess of wild greens without I'd ask him.' They said, 'We didn't know all this.' I said, 'I bet you know it now. I bet you know it now.'"

TOBIAS SCHNEEBAUM

# *A Drive*
# *into the Unknown*

Scenes from my past sometimes cry out for description. They come back to me time and again, demanding to be put onto the printed page, as if the experiences return to my conscious mind solely to be recorded. Their return also forces me to renew my acquaintance with old friends and to exorcise old demons. Printed on the page, the scenes take on new reality and I relive them to the full, sometimes taking myself deeper into the event than I had originally gone. Everything suddenly becomes more vivid and I look back and think, How did I dare?

Typical of these revisited moments is an incident that took place when I was collecting artifacts and information for a small museum in Asmat, a remote area of what used to be called Netherlands New

Guinea and is now a part of Indonesia called Irian Jaya, where, altogether, I spent more than four years. On this occasion I was staying in the village of Basim, when six men from the upstream village of Buepis paddled down the Fayit River to see what I was doing. After the usual amenities I asked whether they had any ancestor skulls or trophy heads that they were willing to trade for. Yes, they said, there were some in their village. I told them I wanted only those which were decorated in traditional style and that I wouldn't buy any skulls that had just been dug up to sell. The men agreed and said they would return in a few days.

My six paddlers arrived early on the specified morning and loaded my trade goods in their canoe. The tide was coming in fast, and we rode up to Buepis. There we were received with great enthusiasm by the village men; the women were still out fishing. As I got out of the canoe the men lifted and carried me into the men's house. They chanted and yelped. They carried my two aluminum patrol boxes and the goods that didn't fit inside; there was plenty of tobacco, nylon, fishhooks, razor blades, machetes, steel axes and small steel knives. I sat against a wall made of sago leaf ribs and the men sat in front of me, watching my every move. From the smaller aluminum box I took two plugs of spiced tobacco and put them in front of the chief. He reached forward and broke the tobacco into small sections, which he distributed to the men, who rolled it in nipah leaves.

A decorated skull was brought in, the jawbone tied to the rest of the skull with rattan, the nose hole and the eyes stuffed with beeswax that was embedded with coix and abrus seeds. Over the forehead and the back of the skull was a netting of seeds and white cockatoo feathers. It was a good example of what I was looking for. I put out an ax blade, a machete, some rolls of nylon, a box of fishhooks and a plug of tobacco — an inevitable part of every exchange. Everyone approved of what I offered for the skull; I was giving more than they expected. The men were excited and began to move in and out of the building, bringing in other artifacts: drums, necklaces from which hung the feet of flying foxes or the black dried penises of wild boars, or which were made of human hair and human teeth, of dog teeth, of the inner sections of the chambered nautilus shell, of seeds and feathers and the atlas bone of the human neck, the latter a necklace indicating that the wearer had taken a head in battle.

More skulls were brought in, one by one, each more beautiful than the last, the next skull appearing only after the men were satisfied that I had paid properly for the previous one. The men were smok-

ing furiously, puffing deeply and as quickly as possible. I traded for seven beautifully decorated heads,
two of which were trophy skulls, easily identified as
such because they were missing the jawbone and had
a hole in the temple through which the brains had
been extracted. (Usually the jawbone was used as the
centerpiece of a woman's necklace.) After a while I
had dozens of necklaces, drums, food bowls, paint
bowls, bowls made of sago leaf into which brains had
once been poured, and other artifacts.

Hours later, when I had bought everything of
interest to me that they offered, I began packing the
remains of my goods.

"Why are you packing that tobacco and the other
things?" asked the chief. "That has to stay here."

"I'm taking it back to Basim," I said.

"Oh, no you're not! That tobacco belongs to us.
You know we share everything in Asmat. Give me
the tobacco!"

"You're not getting it," I said. "I'm taking it with
me."

"No you won't," countered the chief. "It belongs
to us!" The men were angry and getting angrier, and
the angrier they got, the angrier I got. The men stood
up, raised their fists and pushed their bare chests into
me, almost knocking me down.

I looked at those faces, some painted, some with human bones or spiraled shells through their noses, and began to shout: "Listen, I have been here more than four hours and you never once offered me anything to eat. Nothing! Is that the way the Asmat act? No sago! No shrimp! No pig meat! And you expect me to leave tobacco here? Never! I have never before left a village like this with hunger in my stomach."

I could see that all the men were looking at one another shamefacedly. "Now," I said, "I want everything that I gave you returned to me immediately. I want my machetes and my axes and my fishhooks back. You can keep your skulls. I want everything back."

I called out to my paddlers, who had already packed my purchases in the canoe, to bring it all back. They came into the men's house with the skulls and other pieces. There was a nervous laugh from the chief, and the other men also laughed nervously. It was obvious that I was serious and angry. The chief said, "Oh, Tobias, we were joking. You didn't think we would take your goods, did you? It was a joke! We were only kidding." Everyone began hugging me and jumping up and down. "It was just a joke," they all said.

The men carried me back to the canoe. By the time we were waving goodbye, everyone was again in good humor, except me.

All this time I had been recording data about the artifacts, writing in my journal everything I could learn: the names of the men whose skulls were then in my possession; who sold them to me; their relationship with the deceased; how each man died (invariably through magic, in the case of the ancestor skulls); the names, in Asmat, of the seeds and feathers; and how string was made from *fum*, the inner bark of the paper mulberry tree, the same material that tapa cloth is made from in the South Pacific. I tried to get information on the symbolism of the designs, but was often frustrated, since the men were reluctant to reveal secrets to any outsiders, whether white or Asmat from another village.

My journal was always with me, and I wrote up the day's events as quickly as possible, knowing that even the most important happenings can easily be forgotten. The journal calmed me and forced me to think clearly about the day. Often the day had been muddled with so many things happening one after another that the only way to straighten it out was to write about it, reliving it until the pattern of incidents sorted itself out. Recording specific information had to be done as soon as it was learned, and this gave me a kind of chart that later helped to trigger the circumstances I wanted written down.

My attitude on a given day was often reflected in my manner of writing, surprising me when I later reread it. In Basim that night when I returned from Buepis I was still upset by the final confrontation with the men, and, looking into the journal now, I see that my handwriting is almost illegible because of the anger I still felt so many hours afterward.

People often ask me if I've been afraid on these trips, and my answer is always never. The fear comes only after the fact, when I've thought it over or when I'm writing in my journal.

A good example of this took place in 1976, when I was invited by a surveying company looking for oil in the untouched territory in the foothills of the Jayawijaya Mountains, east of Asmat, to do some museum collecting. The company had been hired by an international oil conglomerate, and its manager hoped I would write something positive about what they were doing. I saw nothing positive, unless you count the pork chops, steaks, fresh fruit and other victuals that were flown in daily from Darwin. On the other hand, I saw the devastation of gardens and houses and large sections of the forest. I also heard from American helicopter pilots and Australians about the local people who had been shot because they were trying to protect their land and houses.

The Australians supervised the Indonesian workmen cutting the narrow pathways—or "lines"—through the jungle, each line many kilometers in length. Behind the men who slashed at the jungle were other workmen digging holes in the swamp and planting one-pound sticks of dynamite. Two men then set off the dynamite and registered the sound waves on a seismographic device that recorded the waves to a depth of five thousand feet. The resulting graph, which was sent to Jakarta for analysis, provided information on the consistency of the soil and in turn indicated whether or not there might be oil. The lines were cut west to east and south to north, forming a gigantic grid. It didn't matter what was in the way; the lines were cut perfectly straight, all too often destroying gardens of bananas, taro, cassava and other root vegetables as well as knocking down houses.

The people of the area, the Kombai and the Koroway, had never seen outsiders before and resented the invasion of their territory. The hamlets that they lived in were small, with fifteen or twenty men, women and children. The houses were perched high on stilts or tree trunks, eighteen to thirty-five feet above the ground. When the invaders approached,

the local people put magic signs across the encroach-
ing line — human skulls and spears — hoping to
frighten the outsiders away. But nothing daunted the
soldiers or policemen who were there to protect the
workmen. They had heard that the people were
headhunters and cannibals and they never hesitated
to shoot anyone who came into sight, armed or
unarmed.

The Australian man who managed the surveying
company from its base camp in Senggo, far downstream, had given me the freedom to travel and to use
company equipment as long as I didn't interfere with
the work or the workmen. I went alone in the outboard, my boat loaded with food and trade goods, to
search for the people who had killed four Indonesian
policemen who had shot two obviously domesticated
pigs. A couple of hours upstream I saw a young man
standing at the edge of the Brazza River, his flexed
arrow pointed at me. He didn't shoot as I came
closer. I was naked in the aluminum boat, hoping, as
always, that my nakedness among men who were
naked would show my vulnerability and prove that I
had no weapons. When I got nearer, however, I
could see that the young man was not naked but was
wearing a penis leaf. He accepted the tobacco I
offered and then came down into the boat. His name,
he said, was Yosigipi.

He led me to a great house in which some forty people lived. Around the huge open room I saw evidence of the policemen who had been killed: a leather belt, a shirt, a pair of boots. I stayed there a week, thoroughly enjoying myself under the protection of Yosigipi, who was the son of the chief. I collected twelve shields and some smaller artifacts and then returned to the base at Senggo. After that I went out on the lines on several occasions, each time for four or five days, sometimes meeting Kombai people on one of their trails when I was completely alone.

I had been a guest of the surveying company for about two months when Brad, one of the American helicopter pilots, came to me after he had seen a huge house and some other structures being built in the jungle. He wanted me to help him take a closer look. Late one afternoon I took off with Brad and with Jack, another American pilot, who had been designated my bodyguard because I had no company insurance. Again, I was naked.

Brad pointed ahead to a clearing in the forest, where men and women were running in all directions, terrified of the monstrous animal that was flying down on them. The thatch roofing of one of the houses flew up in the wind of the rotary blades but didn't detach itself. We had taken off the doors of the chopper to facilitate jumping out, since there was no place to land. The area was covered with the trunks of trees that had been cut down to open the jungle for the houses. I threw out the machetes, the steel axes and the patrol box that I had brought along. The chopper flew down to fifteen feet above the ground. I jumped out and Jack followed. My arrangement with Brad had been for him to hover at one hundred feet and wait to see whether the people attacked us or were friendly. If they were friendly he would fly off and return in a couple of days. If they attacked us he would come right down, drop a rope, and we would climb back up into the chopper.

On the ground, Jack and I waited a few minutes, but it was clear that nobody would come out of hiding while the helicopter was above us. I signaled to Brad to go back to camp, and he flew away. Slowly the men came out — two or three, then another two or three, until there were fifty or sixty men in the distance. The men began walking toward us along the logs, approaching faster and faster, yelling in a tongue unknown to me. I shouted back, "Don't be afraid!" I waved a machete, hoping they would understand that I was offering it to the first man to reach me. The men kept coming. They would run ten steps forward, turn, and run five steps back, always yelping and screeching. The men shot arrows that landed short or flew over our heads. There was a tremendous hullabaloo.

Half an hour later the men were close enough for me to see that they wore various decorations in and around their noses. Most of them wore the second wing bone of the flying fox sticking straight up from their nostrils. All had dozens of coix seeds set around their nares, embedded in the skin. Their earrings were of bamboo — hollow plugs in which they carried dried moss to start fires with. They wore necklaces of cuscus teeth and wild boar teeth but were otherwise naked. Their hair was shaved high above the forehead. I remember these details because I was trying to imprint the scene in my head so that I could put it in my journal later.

The noise was deafening. The men were about fifteen feet away when one of them broke from the mass, grabbed my machete and ran back to be absorbed into the group. When they saw that I didn't try to get it back they let out a great *whoop!* A few of the men came up to me and laughed, jumped up and down, and hugged me. Suddenly I heard a voice cry out: "Tobias, let's get out of here! They're going to kill us!" It was Jack. Then he cried out again: "Damn! I shit in my pants!"

When the hullabaloo died down, Jack took off his

pants and washed them in a nearby stream. Then we went into the men's house. Taro and fish were brought in and cooked. I traded for artifacts and collected some drums, shields and smaller pieces. During our stay we never saw a woman. As always, in Asmat and in the surrounding area the women were more afraid of outsiders than the men were and hid themselves and their children against the possibility of the evil eye being cast on them. In general they were shy of strangers and would never talk openly to a man who wasn't in the immediate family, for fear of being accused of adultery and beaten by their husband. It was also common practice for neighboring tribes to capture women and keep them as childbearing slaves.

After two days the helicopter returned and the men again disappeared, undoubtedly watching from their hiding places. We climbed a rope into the chopper and flew back to camp. Jack told the story to everyone, admitting that in his fear he had lost control of his bowels. By that confession he proved, at least to himself and his friends, that our situation had indeed been hair-raising.

What interests me about the story is that it shows two points of view of one experience: Jack was terrified, I was thrilled. At base camp everyone was scared of the local people, although they had never had any contact with them. Australians, Americans and Indonesians from other islands had all listened to and repeated stories of cannibalism and headhunting with great enthusiasm; in fact, these myths circulated continually, the storyteller working his listeners to a feverish pitch with astonishing versions of tales that needed no embroidering. It wouldn't do simply to describe the details of the death of the four Indonesian policemen — that the bodies of two of them had been found floating downstream and that the other two had disappeared completely. Instead I heard of mutilations and missing limbs and munched flesh.

The truth is that confusion and exaggeration reigned. Jack had expected us to be killed — violence is the only thing he saw in the men during our confrontation. Back at the camp, he showed me the pistol that he had taken along, hidden in one of his boots, but that he had fortunately forgotten about in his terror. If he had remembered and used the pistol we surely would have been killed.

Later, writing of this episode in my journal and reliving those incredible hours made me remember the journal of Captain Cook. In it he describes two boatloads of his men attempting a landing on the south coast of Asmat. The men were so frightened by a meeting similar to ours that they shot off their rifles and killed many people, thus beginning a long history of violence between visitors and the Asmat. Cook's experience is only one example of what were innumerable encounters over the centuries of exploration in what we call primitive lands. Cultures vary, experience varies, and conflict is, sadly, almost inevitable.

I have a need to travel to distant corners of the world. At times a yearning comes over me, an urgency to rid myself of the vestments of civilization, to find a new kind of freedom, one not found at home. I don't know what that freedom is or what I'm searching for. I only know it as a drive within me into the unknown. Living with the Asmat seemed to satisfy and fulfill me, though the Asmat code of behavior and sense of morality is, in its own way, just as restrictive as our own, narrow-minded in ways we can't imagine or invent. I also have a need to share my experiences, to let people know that there are other ways of living.

I keep my journal almost as a confessional. I speak of my innermost thoughts, my secrets, my joys, my difficulties, my sexual life, my feelings for my Asmat friends and lovers, and my feelings about the missionaries and the oil company. After reading and rereading it I evoke experiences down to the last detail.

My journal is also my way of record-keeping and of learning languages. I write descriptions of people, landscapes, feasts, myths and the meanings of all that I am part of. More often than not, the journal is distracting, for it takes away from the immediacy of the situation in which I am involved. A tape recorder is no help — the men are fearful of its presence. I try to take notes casually, even surreptitiously, but in vain. Nobody asks what I'm doing, but they wonder at my scribbles, and when I draw motifs they are fascinated. They take my pen and paper and draw, but their vision is in carving, and the pen makes little sense to them. Yet I feel them coming closer and closer to me.

During my first year in Asmat I had no sense of physical balance. Gradually I learned to walk barefoot over thin, slippery logs that were bridges over streams and ditches, and I learned to stand and paddle in a canoe. This was a big step, for it meant that I no longer had to sit in the bottom like a woman. Women have the same extraordinary sense of balance as the men, but generally they sit to paddle.

Standing in the canoe, with three or four men in front of me and three or four in back, gave me an astonishing feeling of freedom and was far less constraining than sitting. We went long distances up narrow rivers with branches and foliage arching

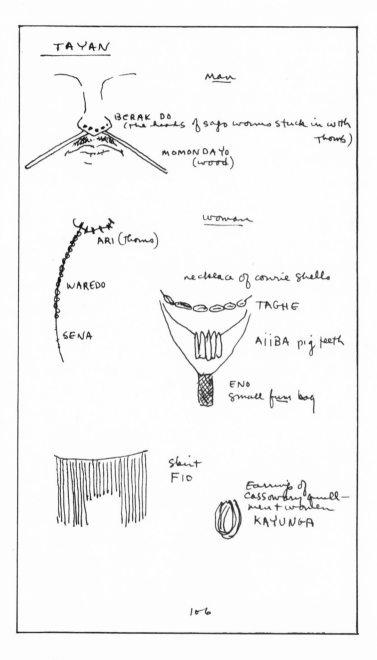

TAYAN

Man

BERAK DO
(the heads of sago worms stuck in with thorns)

MOMONDAYO
(wood)

woman

ARI (thorns)

WAREDO

SENA

necklace of cowrie shells

TAGHE

AiiBA pig teeth

ENO
small fur bag

skirt
FIO

Earring of cassowary quill — men + women
KAYUNGA

106

overhead. Vines of flames-of-the-woods hung down with great clusters of scarlet blossoms; bromeliads and orchids and all manner of epiphytes and parasites clustered in the crotches of trees and along living branches, and saprophytes grew on rotting tree trunks. The silence, except for the bird calls in the early morning and evening, was intense, pressing into me and filling me with joy. It was then that I would think back over the day's events and the possibilities of the next day. I recalled as much as I could of what I would put into my journal and then wrote it down. The air was filled with energy that revitalized me and even took me back to music I had heard at the Metropolitan Opera House and Carnegie Hall. I would hear Callas singing Norma, her voice coming from all directions.

The first time I arrived in Bisus I was in a canoe with four paddlers. The village was hardly more than a house or two. The people had no contact with outsiders but were friendly and delighted to see one of the strangers they had heard many tales about. I spent a night there, made friends and collected shields and other artifacts. The men had no metal and were still using stone axes and adzes. I traded steel for stone, always adding a plug of tobacco and a variety of fishhooks and nylon. Then I went on with my paddlers and met other people and traded again, always taking notes on everything I bought and making drawings of designs. I spent part of every evening with my journal.

I am greedy while I'm collecting. For me, that's the most important time with the objects; once I have catalogued them in the museum they are no longer mine, and all I retain is the information I gathered. I was especially interested in the villages of the foot-hills because the people continued to live in a traditional way, with no influence from the outside world. Their war shields were different in shape and design from the shields of other areas.

In the early 1980s I learned that the oil company was about to start drilling at Bisus. A town was established with prefabricated houses and most of the amenities of Western civilization. Bulldozers knocked down the forest and helicopters flew in and out constantly with Australians and Americans. Great electric lamps glared throughout the night and the noises of drilling were heard twenty-four hours a day. I imagined the astonishment of the people of Bisus, living a few meters away. Six months passed and nothing was found but water. There was no oil. The company abandoned the site and took everything with it, leaving not one wooden board or stick of furniture. Except for the barren space at the edge of the river, there was no indication rafters. Hanging items of all kinds, lots of bundles of TISAN, net bags, baskets with drying tobacco, possibly pandanus leaves hanging to dry for cigarette paper, several types of unknown leaves in bundles, pipes, crocodile skulls, cuscus skins (black, brown, striped, mixed). Some men with shorts, most naked, no women, some men with a single string around corona of penis, one with a narrow rattan band. Only a few men around, tho obviously the house held at least 20 families. We are told that ahead are the villages of: SURABI, SIPANAM, BIAPIS.

TAMDAKA

It takes one hour and 35 minutes to reach SURABI. Half an hour up, we come to a division in the river, too shallow for us to go on in the mappi. SURABI had good shield. Bought three. Four are still there, but the owners were not home. There's a small protestant church in the center of the village. Men still wear the large curved pig bones in their nose.

We stopped at 4 pm at the junction of a river going off to the left. On the map it looks like it connects back below the SIRETSI and forms an island. Al, Ed and I went in the outboard up the SIRETSI as far as we could go, an hour upstream where there were too many trees and logs for us to continue on. We got out of the outboard and walked along the rocky beach but could not find a way through that would not be dangerous. We saw some sukun but no sago. We went downstream for a few minutes and then went up a river on the right (going downstream) and continued on for half an hour but although we saw some signs of human activity — a path, a few banana trees, there was no canoe or bridge. We went beyond the banana trees but found nothing, turned around, and went back to the mappi, arriving just at 6 pm, a bit late for my taste, since it is already pretty dark. When we approached SURABI, the men came out and danced their excitement, jumping up and down with their knees out their legs shaping a diamond. Some of the men had Mohawk Indian-type haircut, a fringe running through the center of the head from forehead back to the neck. At all times, though they were friendly enough, the men carried their bows and arrows while with us, as if afraid of attack. This is the first village in which the shields were out in the open, in the houses, one with 3, one with two, and two each with one. The shields were all old and well used. 81

that anyone had been there. Soon the forest re-claimed its property. The devastation that the com-pany caused seems now to have had no meaning, and the people didn't profit by so much as a handful of nails.

This story took me back thirty-five years to my journal of the experiences that resulted in my first book, *Keep the River on Your Right*, when I was living with the Akarama in the Madre de Dios of Peru — another group that had never been contacted by outsiders. They were a wonderfully gentle people with me but, again, were violent under violent cir-cumstances. In fact, it took twelve years — twelve years after my return to the United States — for me to begin to exorcise the demons that possessed me from the moment I left Peru. Without my journal to reread, without the letters I wrote to friends at the time, I couldn't have done any factual writing. The journal allowed me to relive a time that had troubled me deeply because I had been seeing myself as a murderer, seeing myself within one of the Akarama, taking a spear in hand and plunging it into a living human being. In my journal, however — in one ses-sion of returning to the past — I saw the truth. I saw that I was not guilty of murder, that I had committed no crime and had done nothing more than accom-pany friends on a raid in which men were killed. I had taken no active part in the raid and hadn't even known where we were going when we left the village. After reading the journal twelve years later, my life changed. I felt free again, and my book — the story of my life with the Akarama — poured out of me, almost a chapter a week.

Not long after that I learned that the Akarama, like the Asmat, had been accosted by commercial enterprise, by men building a road across Brazil and Peru. They are gone now, all dead, killed by bullets, by fire, by bombs, because they were in the way of bulldozers clearing a path through the forest.

My second book, *Wild Man*, was written more or less on order — my editor suggested that I write a book about my travels. I had nothing to work from except my memory and a few letters that friends had returned to me. I began with a brief account of my early life and then recalled various trips I had made: to Bali, to the island of Nias, to the Sahara, which I crossed from Libya to Chad in the back of a truck, and to other regions of the world where I had spent some time. For me the book was a disaster, although I didn't know that until I reread it a year or two after it was published. If I had worked from a journal I might have turned it into something more cohesive, more interesting. At least I would have had a perspective on the writing itself.

*Wild Man* is the only book that troubles me in what I call my autobiographical trilogy; it's a book I would like to rewrite, expanding some parts and deleting others. By contrast, the book I wrote about my time with the Asmat, *Where the Spirits Dwell*, remains a happy achievement because it grew out of the detailed journal that I kept during those years. Even today the Asmat is an almost inexhaustible source for my writing. I think of the people, my friends, almost daily, no longer with a yearning to return, but simply reminiscing about exciting times and trying to give other people the feeling of what it was like.

# Bibliography

When we were planning this series of talks it occurred to us that we would like to know what books or other sources our authors remembered or consulted or somehow found helpful in writing their own works of travel, and we asked them for an informal list. This bibliography is their answer to our request.

## IAN FRAZIER

These are some of the books I enjoyed reading as I learned about the Great Plains:

Abbott, E. C. ("Teddy Blue"), and Helena Huntington Smith. *We Pointed Them North: Recollections of a Cowpuncher*. New York, 1939.

Adams, Andy. *The Log of a Cowboy*. Boston, 1903.

Anderson, William Marshall. *The Rocky Mountain Journals of William Marshall Anderson*, edited by Dale L. Morgan and Eleanor Towles Harris. San Marino, Calif., 1967.

Audubon, Maria R., and Elliot Coues. *Audubon and His Journals*. New York, 1899.

Bonner, T. D. *The Life and Adventures of James P. Beckwourth*. Minneapolis, 1965.

Bowden, Charles. *Killing the Hidden Waters*. Austin, 1977.

Brininstool, E. A. *Crazy Horse, the Invincible Ogalalla Sioux Chief*. Los Angeles, 1949.

Brisbin, Gen. James S. *The Beef Bonanza; or, How to Get Rich on the Plains*. Philadelphia, 1881.

Carrington, Mrs. Margaret I. *Absaraka, Home of the Crows*. Chicago, 1950.

Chardon, Francis A. *Chardon's Journal at Ft. Clark 1834–1839*, edited by Annie Heloise Abel. Pierre, S.D., 1932.

Chittenden, Hiram M. *The American Fur Trade of the Far West*. New York, 1935.

Clark, Robert A., editor. *The Killing of Chief Crazy Horse: Three Eyewitness Views*. Glendale, Calif., 1976.

Coakley, Mary Lewis. *Mister Music Maker, Lawrence Welk*. New York, 1958.

Connell, Evan S. *Son of the Morning Star*. San Francisco, 1984.

Cook, John R. *The Border and the Buffalo*. Chicago, 1938.

Custer, Elizabeth Bacon. *"Boots and Saddles"; or, Life in Dakota with General Custer*. Norman, Okla., 1961.

———. *Following the Guidon*. Norman, Okla., 1966.

———. *Tenting on the Plains; or, General Custer in Kansas and Texas*. New York, 1889.

Custer, Gen. George A. *My Life on the Plains*, edited by Milo M. Quaife. Lincoln, Neb., 1966.

Denig, Edwin Thompson. *Five Indian Tribes of the Upper Missouri*, edited by John C. Ewers. Norman, Okla., 1961.

DeVoto, Bernard. *Across the Wide Missouri*. Boston, 1947.

Dimsdale, Prof. Thomas J. *The Vigilantes of Montana; or, Popular Justice in the Rocky Mountains*. Butte, Mont., 1915.

Dobie, J. Frank. *The Longhorns*. Boston, 1941.

Dodge, Richard Irving. *The Plains of the Great West and Their Inhabitants*. New York, 1877.

Durham, Philip, and Everett L. Jones. *The Negro Cowboys*. New York, 1965.

Edwards, William B. *The Story of Colt's Revolver: The*

*Biography of Col. Samuel Colt.* Harrisburg, Penn., 1953.

Emmons, David M. *Garden in the Grasslands.* Lincoln, Neb., 1971.

Ewers, John C. *Indian Life on the Upper Missouri.* Norman, Okla., 1968.

Fehrenbach, T. R. *Comanches: The Destruction of a People.* New York, 1974.

Fischer, John. *From the High Plains.* New York, 1978.

Gard, Wayne. *The Great Buffalo Hunt.* Lincoln, Neb., 1968.

Gatland, Kenneth W. *Missiles and Rockets.* New York, 1975.

Georgia, Ada E. *A Manual of Weeds.* New York, 1914.

Grinnell, George Bird. *The Fighting Cheyennes.* Norman, Okla., 1956.

Harris, Edward. *Up the Missouri with Audubon: The Journal of Edward Harris*, edited by John Francis McDermott. Norman, Okla., 1957.

Howard, Joseph Kinsey. *Montana: High, Wide, and Handsome.* Lincoln, Neb., 1983.

Hunter, John Marvin, and Noah H. Rose. *The Album of Gunfighters.* Bandera, Tex., 1951.

Hyde, George E. *Spotted Tail's Folk: A History of the Brulé Sioux.* Norman, Okla., 1961.

————. *Red Cloud's Folk: A History of the Oglala Sioux Indians*. Norman, Okla., 1937.

Irving, Washington. *A Tour on the Prairies*. Norman, Okla., 1962.

James, Edwin. *Account of an Expedition from Pittsburgh to the Rocky Mountains in the Years 1819, 1820*. London, 1823.

Johnson, Vance. *Heaven's Tableland: The Dust Bowl Story*. New York, 1947.

Kurz, Rudolph Friedrich. "Journal of Rudolph Friedrich Kurz," edited by J. N. B. Hewitt, translated by Myrtis Jarrell, in *Bulletin of the Smithsonian Institution Bureau of American Ethnology*, 115: 1937.

Lamar, Howard R. *The Reader's Encyclopedia of the American West*. New York, 1977.

Lame Deer, John Fire, and Richard Erdoes. *Lame Deer, Seeker of Visions*. New York, 1976.

Larpenteur, Charles. *Forty Years a Fur Trader on the Upper Missouri*. Chicago, 1933.

Laubin, Reginald, and Gladys Laubin. *The Indian Tipi: Its History, Construction and Use*. Norman, Okla., 1957.

Leonard, Zenas. *Leonard's Narrative*, edited by W. F. Wagner. Cleveland, 1904.

Lewis, Meriwether. *Original Journals of the Lewis and

*Clark Expedition, 1804–1806,* edited by Reuben Gold Thwaites. New York, 1959.

Marquis, Thomas B. *Wooden Leg, a Warrior Who Fought Custer.* Lincoln, Neb., 1957.

Mayer, Frank H., and Charles B. Roth. *The Buffalo Harvest.* Denver, 1958.

McKee, Russell. *The Last West: A History of the Great Plains of North America.* New York, 1974.

McLaughlin, James. *My Friend the Indian.* Seattle, 1970.

Miller, Nyle H., and Joseph W. Snell. *Great Gunfighters of the Kansas Cowtowns.* Lincoln, Neb., 1967.

Munford, Kenneth. *John Ledyard: An American Marco Polo.* Portland, Ore., 1939.

Parkman, Francis. *The Oregon Trail.* New York, 1978.

Putnam, Carleton. *Theodore Roosevelt: A Biography.* New York, 1958.

Reisner, Marc. *Cadillac Desert: The American West and Its Disappearing Water.* New York, 1986.

Rich, E. E. *Hudson's Bay Company 1670–1870.* New York, 1961.

Ruxton, George Frederic. *Life in the Far West.* New York, 1849.

Sandoz, Mari. *Crazy Horse.* Lincoln, Neb., 1961.

———. *Old Jules.* Boston, 1935.

Schuchert, Charles. *O. C. Marsh, Pioneer in Paleontology*. New Haven, 1940.

Sharp, Paul F. *Whoop-Up Country: The Canadian-American West 1865–1885*. Minneapolis, 1955.

Siringo, Charles. *A Texas Cowboy; or, Fifteen Years on the Hurricane Deck of a Spanish Pony*. Lincoln, Neb., 1979.

Smith, Charles Henry. *The Coming of the Russian Mennonites*. Berne, Ind., 1927.

Stearn, E. Wagner, and Allen E. Stearn. *The Effect of Smallpox on the Destiny of the Amerindian*. Boston, 1945.

Stegner, Wallace. *Wolf Willow: A History, a Story, and a Memory of the Last Plains Frontier*. Lincoln, Neb., 1980.

Stuart, Granville. *Forty Years on the Frontier*. Cleveland, 1925.

Toole, K. Ross. *The Rape of the Great Plains: Northwest America, Cattle and Coal*. Boston, 1976.

Tweton, D. Jerome. *The Marquis de Morès: Dakota Capitalist, French Nationalist*. Minneapolis, 1972.

Vestal, Stanley. *Sitting Bull, Champion of the Sioux*. Norman, Okla., 1957.

———. *New Sources of Indian History 1850–1891*. Norman, Okla., 1934.

Webb, Walter Prescott. *The Great Plains*. New York, 1931.

Wedel, Waldo R. *Prehistoric Man on the Great Plains.* Norman, Okla., 1961.

Wied-Neuwied, Maximilian Alexander Philipp. *Travels in the Interior North America in the Years 1832 to 1834,* translated by H. Evans Lloyd. London, 1843.

Wright, Robert M. *Dodge City: The Cowboy Capital.* Wichita, Kan., 1913.

## MARK SALZMAN

I'm embarrassed to admit that this short bibliography pretty much represents all the travel books I know. It's not that I have anything in particular against travel writing; I'm just not very well read. One strike against travel writing, though, is that many writers who describe familiar places without making shallow or trite observations suddenly run into trouble when they go abroad. They seem to lose their inhibitions when they find themselves in exotic surroundings, and start telling us how red-cheeked and healthy the children look, how much more in touch with nature Third World farmers appear, or how dull-witted the natives look because they stare at foreigners with their mouths hanging open. Part of the fun of being a traveler is making broad generalizations from what little you see and hear, or discovering that there is a grain of truth in many cultural stereotypes, but those sorts of insights don't necessarily belong in a book.

Anyway, here is a list of travel literature that I've enjoyed a lot. Not everything on my list is a book, and not all of it is nonfiction. I live dangerously.

*Out of Africa*, by Isak Dinesen. Occasional boring descriptions of landscape and so on, but hang in there. Not for nothing was it made into a Meryl Streep movie.

*The Village of Waiting*, by George Packer. George was in the Peace Corps in Togo while I was in China. Very sad but very moving, and great writing.

*Never Cry Wolf*, by Farley Mowat. Not so much a sense of people as a sense of wolves, but what a sense of wolves! Mr. Mowat lived near a pack of them way up in the Arctic for almost a year, and even ate and slept like the wolves, to give as accurate a report of their behavior as possible. He even gives you his recipe for pan-fried tundra mice.

*The Forest People*, by Colin Turnbull. Daily life with a small band of Pygmies in the forest of central Africa. Some aspects of their lives seem remarkably similar to our own, but other aspects seem magical and otherworldly. You simply have to read Turnbull's description of the *molimo*, a forest spirit that sings to the Pygmies in the middle of the night.

*Discos and Democracy*, by Orville Schell. A collection of essays about the democracy movement in China and some of the bizarre ways that Westernization had affected China by the late 1980s.

*Kon-Tiki*, by Thor Heyerdahl. A trip from Peru to the South Seas on a balsa raft with the Nordic master of understatement. He catches six-foot sharks by reaching out and grabbing their tails as they swim by, then holds them upside down until they lose consciousness.

*The Long Ships*, by Frans Bengtsson. Speaking of Norsemen, this is a novel about the adventures of Red Orm, an eleventh-century Viking, written by a Swedish historian. Based largely on fact, this is my favorite travel story. If you like martini-dry humor and lots of old-fashioned gore, you'll love this book. To give you some idea, here is a chapter title: "Concerning the strangers that came with salt, and how King Sven lost a head."

*For All Mankind*, a movie about the Apollo moon shots. Just one of many unforgettable moments: The capsule is orbiting the earth with its camera pointed out the rear when suddenly the rockets fire, sending the capsule toward the moon. Without gravity and air drag to slow it down, the capsule accelerates as if shot out of the barrel of a gun, and almost instantly speeds up to something like twenty thousand miles an hour. It happens so fast you can actually see the earth start to get smaller. Think about that when you're stuck in traffic.

# VIVIAN GORNICK

In Cairo I read a book by Lady Duff Gordon called *Letters from Egypt*. I stumbled on it accidentally in the library of an Egyptian doctor and it became my guide and my companion; it clarified the task for me, made me understand better what it was I was trying to do. Here was an Englishwoman dying of tuberculosis in Luxor at the end of the nineteenth century, sending letters home around the same time that Lord Kitchener was sending his reports back to London. It was the difference between General Westmoreland reporting on Vietnam and Frances FitzGerald writing *Fire in the Lake*. I read Lady Gordon's letters and I believed her. Her Egyptians were real; they reminded me of Egyptians I was meeting every day in Cairo.

I also read the diaries of a French soldier who had been sent to Egypt with the Napoleonic expedition of 1792. This soldier had been quartered in Montsoura (a town now known for its blue-eyed, blond Egyptians). Here he recorded his daily impressions of the natives. As I read the diaries I laughed, I cried, I exclaimed. This could have been written yesterday, I thought, so like my own impressions were his.

After that I read indiscriminately whatever collection of letters, diaries and journals I found written by English or European travelers to Egypt from the eighteenth century on. This was a literature that touched, excited and reassured me. I needed to place myself in it, see where I merged with it, where I departed from it, pay attention to what had been on the mind of someone like me walking a hundred years ago the streets I walked. Every one of these letter writers and diarists was useful and interesting to me, but none was more thoughtful and evocative than Lady Gordon. She remained unrivaled as the traveler who had gone before.

Then there were Alan Moorehead's books on the Nile. I hadn't read them when they appeared piecemeal in *The New Yorker*. Reading them in Egypt, I seemed to inhale them. I responded to the Nile as to no other river I had ever been on, including the Hudson, which I've loved since childhood. From that first morning in Cairo when I walked out onto a stone balcony and there it lay, its waters thick and wide, gray-green, shimmering in the already burning sun, this river—in a place in the world that was hot, brilliant, remote—moved me to a tenderness of feeling from which I never recovered. Every day in Egypt I longed for the Nile, and never more so than when I sat or walked beside it or sailed up it, as I did once, toward the Sudan.

So Alan Moorehead's books recounting the incredible history of nineteenth-century expeditions to the source of the Nile were thrilling to me. And chastening as well. After all, these European explorers, penetrating to the green heart of Africa, about to enslave a continent, had even more romantic feelings about the river than I did.

Then, in Egypt, I reread E. M. Forster's *A Passage to India* and *Pharaohs and Pharillons*, as well as George Orwell's *Burmese Days* and essays out of Africa. These two incomparable Englishmen in what we now call the Third World helped me think about how to use myself to discover Egypt, how to make myself a character among characters, so that the Egyptians could become themselves through me. Forster's intelligence taught me that I must silence the noise within—although this was a lesson that took years to sink in—and Orwell's voice was the beginning of my long apprenticeship at finding my own. I had read them both before, but in Egypt I took them in as though for the first time.

## CALVIN TRILLIN

Several books on specific regions of the country come
to mind — books that talk about not just the way a
place is but also how it got that way: *Night Comes to the
Cumberlands*, by Harry M. Caudill (Atlantic–Little,
Brown, 1962), on Appalachia; *The Super-Americans*,
by John Bainbridge (Doubleday, 1961), on Texas;
*Coming into the Country*, by John McPhee (Farrar,
Straus & Giroux, 1977), on Alaska; *The Mind of the
South*, by W. J. Cash; and such books by C. Vann
Woodward as *The Strange Career of Jim Crow* and *The
Burden of Southern History*, on the states of the Old
Confederacy.

Some American cities have been caught particularly well by novelists. I have spent a lot of time in
New Orleans over the years, and I was astonished at
how perfectly it was captured by Walker Percy in his
first novel, *The Moviegoer*. Oddly enough, two other
first novels also seemed to me successful in catching
the tone of New Orleans: *Hall of Mirrors*, by Robert
Stone, and *A Confederacy of Dunces*, by John Kennedy
Toole.

To my mind, the real stock in trade of superior
mystery writers is a sense of place. I think you can get
a feeling for the Navajo reservation by reading one of
Tony Hillerman's books, just as you can get a feeling

for southern California by reading one of Ross Macdonald's books, or for South Africa by reading the early mysteries of James McClure.

During the years I traveled for the "U.S. Journal" series I accumulated several old books on American cities, and I sometimes consulted the chapter on my destination before I left to do a story. A couple of times I quoted something I had found in the old books. I remember quoting one writer who said that Denver's growth owed so much to its late nineteenth-century reputation as a place with climate beneficial to those suffering from tuberculosis that one of its civic monuments probably ought to be a stone rendering of the tuberculosis bacillus. But even if I didn't use a specific piece of information I found it useful to know what someone in, say, 1947 or — in the case of a book called *Peculiarities of American Cities* — 1884 thought of the place.

Occasionally I consult old travel books before going somewhere to do a travel-magazine piece. The only one I can remember quoting was by a rather severe travel writer of late-Victorian times whose name was listed on title pages as Mrs. Alec Tweedie. The book I read was *Sunny Sicily*, but Mrs. Tweedie was also the author of *Through Finland in Carts* and, before she caught on to the value of a snappy title, *Danish Versus English Butter Making*. One of the lines I quoted from *Sunny Sicily* had a familiar ring for anyone who talks much about travel. Writing in 1904 about the Sicilian resort town of Taormina, Mrs. Tweedie said, "The place is being spoilt."


# TOBIAS SCHNEEBAUM

This is a bibliography (or perhaps a guide) to works that have been helpful to me in my field. Such influences have been so varied and extreme that they hardly make sense to me, let alone to anyone else. It is ludicrous, let's face it, to put the movie *Bomba the Jungle Boy* together with books like Malinowski's *Argonauts of the Western Pacific* or *The Sexual Life of the Savages*, or to put someone like Johnny Ray together with Miles Davis or Shostakovich.

However, if any books can be said to have affected me deeply, two that come immediately to mind are Bernanos's *Diary of a Country Priest* and Wilfred Thesiger's *Arabian Sands*. The loneliness, the search for inner peace, the need for emotional or physical pain, are subjects that speak to me directly. Thesiger's long, splendidly evocative description of crossing the Empty Quarter of Arabia impressed me even more than Doughty's *Arabia Deserta*, partly because of his honesty about his physical discomforts. He traveled for months in intense heat, always with sand everywhere — in his eyes, in his mouth, in his food — always in pain atop his camel or with his feet burning as he walked in hot sand, never comfortable for a moment, but always thrilled and never, he wrote, wishing himself elsewhere. Malinowski, on the other hand, wrote bitterly in his journal about the people he lived with.

Paintings and sculpture influenced me, of course, as did the dance world, the theater and a string of books that impress me now more than ever with their insights and physical descriptions, such as Melville's *Omoo* and *Typee*. And there were certain great films of my youth that I remember vividly: those made by Osa and Martin Johnson; *Trader Horn;* the first *Mutiny on the Bounty; King Solomon's Mines,* and the scenes with painted warriors in the old Tarzan movies.

Now that I think this over, none of these, nor any other works, pushed me in any direction. I was only looking at or reading what I already knew would excite me. The urge to move into distant lands was always with me.

## WILLIAM ZINSSER

My introduction is as much a bibliography as an introduction. It might even be called a bibliography posing as an introduction. It's a lopsided list, serving certain points that I wanted to make but not trying for thoroughness or balance. Europe hardly gets mentioned in the piece, and there's nothing about England, though many wonderful books have been set there, one of my favorites being John Hillaby's *A Walk Through Britain*, an account of a hike from Land's End to John O'Groats. There's nothing — speaking of the British — by V. S. Pritchett, one of the best of travel writers (*The Offensive Traveller*). There's also nothing about big cities, though I'm a lifelong city dweller, as drawn to London and Rome and Hong Kong as I am to Tahiti and Timbuktu. City books are an unusually rich form of the travel genre. Two that I remember with gratitude are John Russell's *Paris* and, of course, E. B. White's *Here Is New York*, the champ.